The Bounce Back Journey

AN INSPIRING COLLECTION OF PERSONAL STORIES

Compiled by
Discover Your Bounce Publishing

"Life is not about how fast you run or how high you climb, but how well you bounce."

TIGGER

CONTENTS

FOREWORD

By Nicky Marshall

In January 2015 I wrote seven words into my journal:

'I am an international author and speaker'

I had no idea how to make this happen.

At this point I had self-published two books and to be honest I think my mum had bought most of the copies! I was proud of my creations and had always loved writing. My love of writing started by entering a poem into a competition at the grand old age of ten and I have been hooked ever since. I got an A grade in my O level, always excelled in the writing elements of my accountancy exams and had several articles published before graduating into writing books.

I was a pretty good speaker too. I had hosted networking events, taught various courses and spoken at several local events. I still got so nervous that I felt sick, but always had a retrospective feeling of satisfaction that made me want to stretch to bigger audiences.

This, however, felt like a big leap. I had no idea how it would be possible, but I had made a lot happen in my 45 years on the planet so far and this felt right.

"Over to you!" I said, speaking to The Universe. I have always believed there is an energy around us, whether you call it God, Goddess, Source or All That Is. The Universe seems to encompass a bit of everything and that was to whom I had addressed my wishes so far!

Life has a habit of being busy. Between a business to run and family life, I had settled into the new year and not given my bold statement a second thought. Until one day I connected with a new Facebook friend because of her views on hair colour – true story!

When I asked her what she did for work she said, "I run a publishing company." When I told her I was a writer she asked if I would like to write a chapter for her next book. It sounded fun and so I agreed. When the book was published in May 2015, it was a bestseller on Amazon within 24 hours. The feeling was amazing!

International Author: tick!

In August 2015 we launched a second book; this time I was the compiler. We brought 24 people together to write their stories of bouncing back. People wrote about bullying, grief, suffering infertility and a host of other life challenges. No two stories were the same and the genuine way everyone wrote made me laugh and cry. Our authors were a mix of family, friends, business contacts and connections on Facebook from around the globe.

The Missing Piece in Bouncing Back was launched on my daughter's birthday and also became an Amazon Bestseller. Watching that book rise through the bestseller charts felt like Christmas – the excitement was palpable!

One of our authors, Laurie invited me to her book launch in Boston, to which I jokingly replied, "Of course! Anywhere else I can speak while I'm in Boston?"

Two days later she had arranged for me to speak at the Novartis Institute of Biomedical Research in Boston and at a ladies network at Harvard University.

International Speaker: tick!

The funny thing about wishes and dreams is that they always come with bonuses. My mum and dad came on that trip and we went via New York, watching a very dear friend star as Lise in An American in Paris.

Since publishing, I have met so many people with their own stories of challenges and bouncing back. I have come to realise that most people have overcome an adversity – be it mental, physical or emotional. I also know beyond doubt that people are amazing and capable of such magic, when given the right tools, the right circumstance and a few words of encouragement.

I have been so inspired by the people I have met that once our publishing company was established (due to another series of synchronicities!), a second book was bound to happen. Readers of the first book said how inspired they were; how a collection of stories was the perfect lift for a dreary day or some light lunchtime relief at work.

In part one you will find ten of our original writers (and me!). Some of them have shared more wisdom and a second book would not have felt the same without them.

In part two are our new authors, who have all written from the heart to pass on their own inspiration and wisdom.

Every person has been honest, open and authentic and I am humbled that they have put their faith in us to publish their words. Writing is in my opinion a way of healing; a cathartic expression that makes sense of and releases our struggles. I hope that by sharing, each author finds a new level of peace and a confidence to step forward with a new vigour.

We know that some of the chapters in this book may be a hard read. The stories may trigger emotional responses from your own life. If you can bear in mind that this journey is happening to another and not you, each author has finished by sharing what they learned and how they moved forward. Every one has found that there is light at the end of the tunnel.

In each chapter are gems of wisdom and threads of knowledge that I hope will filter into your life. If you should ever face a challenge and need to draw on some strength, let the words in this book spur you on to find your own bounce back journey.

PART ONE

AMI MORRISON

Ami is in her late-20s, living in Belfast with her husband and baby. She is currently discovering life as a new mother and navigating the perils of sleep deprivation. In her spare time (if she gets any!) she is a proof-reader and editor for Discover Your Bounce Publishing.

Ami is passionate about creating the life you want and overcoming obstacles, even when they seem impossible.

You can reach Ami through the Discover Your Bounce team: info@discoveryourbounce.com

Giving In But Not Giving Up

Everyone has at least one day in their life that changes everything – Tuesday 30th July 2013 was that day for me. After another day of being dismissed by the medical profession I broke down in tears in Mum's kitchen.

"I give in." I told her. "If someone else wants to fight this battle for me, I won't stop them. I give in. I can't do it myself anymore."

Things change when you give in, sometimes with alarming speed. Within minutes I was white, vomiting and had an emergency appointment booked with a different doctor to my usual one. Within hours I was packing my bags for the hospital and by midnight I'd been admitted with two very serious infections.

Let's back up a bit though, about 6 months to be precise. Although I'd always suffered irregular, painful periods I'd dismissed it as normal and got on with life. It wasn't until January 2013 that things started getting worse – the pain was starting earlier, lasting longer and affecting my daily life more. I was starting to experience other symptoms; back and rib pain, bloating, IBS-like symptoms and extreme fatigue.

This was the start of a 6 month dance with my doctor – at first I was given stronger painkillers, but as the pain started to last all month she moved on to an IBS diagnosis. We went through a number of diet changes, medications and promises of seeing a specialist (the last one never materialised), but nothing was working.

The pain kept getting more intense. By March I was sleeping on the living room floor for 2 hours a night so as not to wake Tom up, spending the rest of my time working out the maximum painkillers I could take and scalding myself with hot water bottles because only the most intense heat could give me relief.

Luckily at this time I was working in Mum's business and she was very accommodating. As long as the work got done it didn't matter if I was curled up in a ball with a hot water bottle strapped to my stomach. Being able to work this way meant I was still able to support myself… most of the time.

Even though nothing was working my doctor insisted on the IBS diagnosis when I went back week after week. Eventually I was given blood tests that showed infection, but nothing was done about it except repeat bloods every two weeks 'to see if it goes away'.

That was how I found myself in a hospital bed, trying not to cry as Mum finally went home at 2am to get some sleep.

The next day I had a scan that revealed two large cysts – 8cms on my right ovary and 5cms on my left ovary. My anatomy was a bit of a jigsaw puzzle, with my ovaries pushed up near my belly button and my womb near-invisible squashed between them. It was a surprise to say the least – I thought I'd just been getting fat!

After a few days on antibiotics to get the infections under control I had exploratory surgery to diagnose the cysts and drain them. It was at this point I was diagnosed with Stage IV Endometriosis – a condition where endometrial cells are found outside the womb, attached to the stomach lining and other organs. It was quite a shock, I can tell you that! It started what has been a 2 year journey of treatment, discoveries, education and healing that I'm still on to this day.

My cysts were so large that they couldn't remove them in the first surgery, so part of my treatment was 3 months on a drug called Zoladex, an implant in your stomach that induces a medical menopause, to shrink them. That experience was a whole story in itself! 4 months later I had my second surgery to remove the cysts and as much of the endometriosis as they could, along with checking my fertility.

When I came round from the anaesthetic my consultant explained they couldn't remove all of the endometriosis – my fallopian tubes were attached to my bowel, which they weren't able to separate. I also got the news we'd been dreading: my tubes were completely blocked, meaning my eggs couldn't get through. At this point there were a few tears before my body shut down. I couldn't cope – I've wanted to be a mother for as long as I can remember, even seeing myself as a second mum to my sister when I was just 2 years old – so I slept for the next 24 hours.

Once I was home it was time to heal in any way I could. I had a coil to slow the re-growth of Endo and I got even more focused on the Endo Diet (which you can read about on my blog The Endo Goddess). I lost a lot of weight in the early days and did everything I could to keep a positive mind-set, but I kept getting pulled back by the infertility. There were reminders everywhere – friends were having children, there were children on the bus, I had to walk through the 'little people' section in Ikea…

I was the woman crying in public at the sight of children and I hated it. My body was letting me down in every sense and it was a very rocky time in our household. Tom has been amazing and has done everything he can to help me from the first symptom through to today, but some things can't be healed by another person.

I breezed through the first half of 2014 thinking I was doing well – I started my own business that was very successful in the early days, most of my pain disappeared and (if you ignored the little people, which I was trying to) I was feeling better in myself.

The further into the year I got, the more I realised the impact of my experiences and illness. I was trying to heal and mask severe depression by putting a plaster on it. I was developing social anxiety as I was too scared my pain would flare up while I was out. My business wasn't doing so well, so I ended up spending more and more time home alone and feeling like I'd lost my sense of self.

All of my pre-Endo hobbies had disappeared, some because I didn't have the energy and others just because. I spent much of my time aimlessly online or watching TV shows to pass time. At this point I gave in once again and resigned myself to 'this is it'. I had an okay life – I went out now and then, I had an amazing family supporting me, I could live with that.

Remember how I said things change when you give in? Well, they do. For me sometimes it's in the most spectacular way possible (and not always in the good sense!). In March 2015 I was taken ill at work – vomiting and a fever that came on very suddenly. I assumed it was a 24 hour stomach bug, but after 5 days of no food and little water I slowly started turning yellow. Uh-oh…

I was admitted to hospital again and after 5 days, LOTS of antibiotics and 2 emergency surgeries I came home without a gallbladder to start the recovery process again. By this point I even doubted my abilities – could I ever have a 'normal' life? Would it just be one illness after another?

What should have been a 2 week recovery turned into a 2 month recovery and even now I'm not back to 100%. This time it's different though. Throughout all of this I've had a strong, stubborn streak that just wouldn't let me quit. I've given in to the help of others, I've given in to the universe, but I've never given up and it took me 2 years to see that.

Now instead of fighting to get 'back to me' I'm discovering who I am – with Endo, without a gallbladder – who is Ami in her current form? What does she like, what does she love? What makes her tired (housework, no joke intended!) and what energises her (spending time with family)? Possibly the scariest step – how will we bring a family of our own into this world? It will be another journey, but it's one we'll take on together.

If I've learned just one thing through all of this, it's that you've got to have your tribe. For some that's family, for others it's friends, but you can't make it through alone.

My family were my cheering squad, believing in me when I couldn't. They were my house elves, cleaning and cooking when I was good for nothing but sleep. They were my army when it was time to fight anyone who wasn't listening to my needs and they were shoulders on the hundreds of times I needed to cry on one. I lost myself in the journey, but they always knew I was in here and they've done everything possible and more to help me back out.

Whether you're going through health problems or just not being heard in your life, my advice is to advocate for yourself. Give in when you need to, but never, ever give up on yourself. Gather your tribe, make your plan of attack and then just **go for it**!

The Difference a Year Makes

In 2015 I wrote about being diagnosed with endometriosis, finding out I was infertile and losing my gallbladder. I was living in Bristol with my then-fiancé, surrounded by family and working out who the 'new' Ami was. Well let me tell you, it's been quite a journey!

The logical place to pick up is in April 2016 when my then-fiancé became my ex. Suffice to say that it was amicable in time and the best thing for both of us. While it's not what this chapter is about, it was the catalyst for everything that has happened since.

I have known my current partner since we were in our teens. We had been best friends for 9 years by the time I left my ex, but we'd never met in person. He lived in Belfast and our relationship had been mostly digital the entire time. It's more common these days, but at the time my friends found it hard to understand. During my breakup he was incredibly supportive; helping me with every stage of the breakup. In June 2016 I hopped on a plane, thinking it was about time we met in person.

The rest, as they say, is history. I've been living in Belfast since August 2016 and we have built a beautiful life here together. So, what have I had to bounce back from? If you read my last chapter, or even had keen eyes during the intro, there was still that pesky infertility business bubbling away in the background. Having been friends for so long, we both knew we wanted children. How many was up for debate, but whether to have any wasn't.

In the early days it was a problem for another time while we got to know each other. We weren't in any rush to become a three when we had only just become a two. But as conversations about marriage started, the question of children came up more and more. We knew In-Vitro Fertilisation (IVF) was the only way (biologically), but when? We weren't sure if we were ready just yet, but NHS wait lists could be up to 2 years long! With this in mind it was decided that we would see a specialist and find out what we had to do.

I organise when I'm stressed and I arrived at our first appointment with a folder full of my medical records, Basal Body Temperature (BBT) and ovulation charts, the works. I won't bore you with the details, but we came away with a plan. The endometriosis had been busy since my last surgery, so the cysts had to be removed and then we'd be placed on the wait list for IVF. It would be 1 year until the surgery and then another year until IVF treatment, IF the cysts didn't grow back in that time...

At this point the reality of my diagnosis hit me all over again. The NHS is great, but sometimes it doesn't work efficiently. I couldn't be on both lists at the same time because if an earlier appointment for IVF became available before my surgery and I didn't take it, I'd lose my place on the list. The chance of the cysts growing back in that time frame was almost certain, meaning I'd be in an endless loop of surgery and no IVF.

I can barely remember the worst of this time. It's a haze of tearful phone calls to family, pacing the flat running circles in my head and cuddling on the sofa with my partner, trying to work out what to do. My health had also taken a turn for the worse as the cysts got bigger. Every period felt like a painful reminder of how impossible my situation was. Curled up in a ball, I felt like my physical pain was an echo of the mental pain I couldn't escape. No IVF without surgery, but no way to time it so that the cysts couldn't grow back. Round and round and round.

Through all of this, Mum was a quiet voice saying, "Get a second opinion." I dismissed it at first. Why pay for someone else to tell us what we already knew? But she kept suggesting, never pushing the issue, until I was ready to fight again. Some of the things the first consultant said just didn't add up and it took a while to be ready to hope again.

My partner and I got engaged in February 2018 and this was one of the things that gave me the strength to move forward with a second opinion. We had never felt so secure as a couple and we wanted to know how we would grow our family when the time came. So that summer we went back to Bristol to see a private consultant and learned that a lot of what the previous doctor had said was false. A plan started to take shape, but it wasn't going to be easy...

The second half of 2018 was a blur of consultant appointments and surgery with the aim of starting IVF on the 28th December 2018. What a way to end the year! Christmas Day was a tearful one as my partner and I were about to be separated for 3 weeks while I flew to Bristol for treatment. He would be joining me for the last 10 days, supporting me through the painful procedures and enduring the "two week wait".

My last appointment before starting treatment was nerve wracking. I was given all of the drugs and needles I needed, along with instructions on how to use them. This was going to be the ultimate test of my severe needle phobia! My mum and partner had offered to do the injections for me, but I knew it was something I had to do myself.

The first time was like a military operation. I had everything lined up on the table and ran through the process dozens of times in my head before doing anything. The pressure of having family around got too much and I asked everyone but Mum to leave the room. It seems dramatic now, but at the time it was my way of coping. The process went smoothly and I even began to feel confident. It didn't hurt as much as I was anticipating and a feeling that I could get through this settled over me.

The next two weeks were a flurry of injections, scans and trying to relax whenever I could. When my partner joined me, we moved into a lovely Airbnb flat right next to the hospital. This saved us the 45 minute car journey for each appointment and gave us some much needed space. In no time at all we were on the final stretch of treatment - eggs were collected and we were sent home to wait and see if it worked.

On day 6 we were called back to have the best quality embryo put back. The procedure was a breeze compared to everything else I'd been through, but I was still scared to move afterwards. They say to carry on with your normal activities (within reason), but I didn't want to do anything to risk a bad outcome. I was still a little sore from earlier procedures anyway, so I retired to the sofa to begin the wait.

When we first returned to Belfast I felt confident and almost certain everything had worked, but as time went on doubts started to creep in. As test day approached, I became convinced it had failed and tested a day early to get it over with. We still had a wedding to plan 6 months away and 2 embryos "on ice" to try again when we were ready, so I just wanted to move on.

The 2 minutes waiting for the results felt as long as the 2 weeks we'd already waited. My partner and I sat on the bed, agreeing to go back and look together. I reached the test first and threw myself into his arms screaming and crying. He was a little confused at first, but then I held up the test - we were having a baby! The next hour was full of phone calls and celebrations, we just couldn't believe it had worked first time.

2019 has been another blur of hospital appointments, this time for antenatal checks and scans. It was far from an easy pregnancy; my morning sickness lasted the first 5 months, ending just in time for us to get married in June.

We had a beautiful ceremony with our closest friends and family there to celebrate with us. A short honeymoon followed and very soon it was time to prepare for our imminent arrival. Plenty of nights were spent in admissions at the maternity hospital as our little Bean kept quiet and hid from me. Always fine, but always a worry too! After being monitored weekly for 13 weeks I was induced at 37 weeks. But that story is a whole new chapter!

On 16th September 2019 Baby Morrison joined our family to make three. Our life has changed drastically this year, from a tearful Christmas in 2018 to a happy Christmas of firsts in 2019. First Christmas as a wife, first Christmas as a mother and first of many happy holidays for years to come. I really couldn't have anticipated the events of this year and if I could, I probably would have had a really long sleep first! However, I wouldn't trade the sleep deprived cuddles for anything.

Now I'm just wondering what 2020 will bring!

BRIAN FAKIR

Brian is an advocate of self-care and wellbeing in the community, works actively in his local one and is well respected by them. In Brian's own words, he's getting on a bit now, still thinks he's 18 and wishes he knew back then what he knows now and took action on it. Brian loves his family. He has three children and six grandchildren who keep him busy, plus his extended business family. Brian loves technology and new innovations. He is currently working on podcasting as a venture and has been known to appear on radio occasionally. Brian is a keynote speaker and speaks at many events throughout the UK.

You can contact him on afreshlysqueezedidea@gmail.com

I'm Not Going To Spend My Life Being A Colour

What colour is success? People have always associated colour with some form of emotion. For example, that person has a sunny disposition indicating yellow for happiness or when the red mist forms indicating anger and green with envy for jealousy. Is there a colour for success? Is success an emotion? YOU might think that success equals desire: 'I desire success'. A desire is formed from an emotion, one that makes you smile, makes your heart beat faster, pushing adrenalin through your body, a bit like a roller coaster at a fun fair. So my question is what colour is success?

Born into a mixed race family, my mother is British and my father is North African. I was born in the 1950s; the seeds of racism had already been sown in America and were permeating the United Kingdom. If you've met me before in my adult life, you will ask ,"What did all that have to do with you?" You will find out how instrumental that part of my life was and how it shaped who I am today.

My parents, bless them, decided that both myself and my sister would escape racism by denomination. We weren't going to be Muslims; we would be Christians, Church of England Baptists. What that didn't do was change my colour or my name.

Throughout my primary, yes would you believe primary school, all the way through secondary school, I endured both physical and verbal racist abuse. The effect that had on me was cataclysmic: my only thoughts were, "This is going to be my life forever." I became very shy, insular, nervous, a bed wetter because of my nerves and I lacked all confidence. Everything was always out of my reach because of the word can't. 'You can't do that' and 'You can't be what you want to be'.

As soon as I was able to read properly I found solace in books. The written word was my saviour. I found something I loved, yet the comments started to roll in. "Always got his head in a book, that boy, why isn't he doing something for himself?"" Authors didn't know who I was or pre-judge me. I was reading words without prejudice. I could lose myself in a world of detectives, sports stars and explorers. I could escape and forget my outside world in a book.

What about friends? Of course I had friends, whether I found them or they found me is unclear; however those friends are still here in my life today and wherever they may be in the world, there is always time for a hello through Social Media. Mostly they were from other mixed race families, not necessarily ethnic origin, but they were Israelis, Italians, Portuguese, Spanish, Russian and a smattering of British friends who didn't have any baggage or were taught that people should be liked whatever their origin.

In high school I was streamed into the higher levels of education because of my intelligence. It soon became evident that due to my own issues, my education path was taking a turn for the worse. I was put into the stream that needed help; a slow learner. This put me right into the hands of my persecutors. My parents would not intervene despite my protestations, unreservedly telling me that I had to fight my own battles. I went further and further into my own despair. I was a failure, academically and personally. How was this possible? I was well read, had great knowledge, but known as a failure. It was fear. Fear of asking questions and fear of rejection because I would be told, "Don't be so stupid" and I failed.

I did as I was told, did everything everyone wanted, got jobs I didn't want and everything else that went with it for the next 15 to 20 years. I fumbled and bumbled my way with no clear direction or guidance.

What about success then? I was, 'a successful failure', the only thing I could comfortably accomplish. That had to change. I read books and magazines and they all ran adverts about becoming your own boss. I dreamt about it and wouldn't dare tell anyone that my dream was to one day be my own boss. That is where it stayed. Being well read, I was good at something: research. I was about to change.

I changed my attitude for success. Initially I thought it was about being a boss, building a business, employing people and making money. To a degree that is true, that is what most people want to do and most do it with degrees of success too. However that was still an unattainable dream for me in that moment. I had work to do first; I had to learn.

With every change I implemented, opportunity presented itself. Here were all the things I couldn't do previously because of the, 'You'll never be good enough' message I'd been given.

I applied to university and was immediately accepted as a mature student. What did I study and more to the point, what couldn't I study? There were no limits. I had a choice. Pandora's Box was now open and taking orders.

I majored in science and discovered subjects that interested me, mainly ones that didn't involve a career path because this was just about fuelling my drive and curiosity. I specialised in Biology, the shape of the Brain and Behaviour plus Geology and rock shapes. These two subjects were about to shape me. I qualified with a BSc, it took a long time balancing work and family life, but it was so worth it.

Work opportunities began to present themselves on their own. I was head hunted for almost every job I've had since. I still dreamt of being my own boss though and I tapped into the knowledgebase of these people I worked for. They saw something in me and I delivered. No longer did I have to hide behind my colour or blame it, I embraced it wholeheartedly.

I figured out how to handle people and make friends with them, how to be interested in them and get them interested in me. My world was turning inside out for the positive. I was bouncing back.

In 2000 my magic opportunity came. I was in a position with no commitments other than to myself and was offered an opportunity to start a business with a friend who I'd been encouraging to do this for months. We put our heart and soul into it, I brought all the things I'd learned from my previous mentors and we soared, always sticking to our roots of not being greedy. Things moved at a rapid pace and one part of the business moved faster than the other. I took the gamble and moved myself away and went solo. It was to be what I call 'divine intervention', because of bitterness another person took my friend's business away from him. He lost everything; home, family and friends.

I took on another business; I used everything I knew from before and continued to learn. I became a success, not financially necessarily, but with people. Unfortunately the economic climate took that business at its peak. People pulled their apron strings, as you would. But I knew I had the wherewithal not to give up.

Walking around Tesco one night, I bumped into my old business partner. We hadn't spoken properly for about three years and that's when he told me what happened. There and then an opportunity was realised. We met and talked for hours. The one thing he said has always stayed with me, "We were friends first and we'll always be friends. Business is business, we might fall out, but that's where it stays". He wanted my help and I needed him for my sanity.

In short, that's where we are today. I have used every opportunity that has come my way to springboard me to where I am now. I have friends around the world; I am respected for what I have to say. I'm a published author, I speak weekly to groups of people about what I do and they listen, to me, interested in what I have to say. I sell my products in five European countries.

I look back at my heroes in the books and comics I read and absorbed myself with; they all had superpowers and wore capes, could detect crime, and save the world. Now I see it as a bit more fundamental. All of my heroes helped people and that is what I really wanted to do. It has now defined who I am and how I've bounced back. Just like the song by David Bowie, "We can be heroes, if just for one day."

'You must know that in any moment a decision you make can change the course of your life forever, the very next person you stand behind in line or sit next to on an airplane, the very next phone call you make or receive, the very next movie you see or book you read or page you turn could be the one single thing that causes the floodgates to open and all of the things you've been waiting for to fall into place'. - Courtesy of *Anthony Robbins*

Behind The Mask – My Brave Face

It probably all began when I was 10 or 11. It could have been before, but I don't have any recollection if it was. It's ok that I didn't know what '*it*' was either, or what '*it*' meant. I was probably 13 or 14 when I did understand what '*it*' was.

As I said, I was born into a mixed-race family in 1957. My mother was White, my father of North African descent. My knowledge or experience of racism was minimal. In retrospect, I don't think I ever knew of my parent's exposure to racist behaviour themselves; not that we ever spoke about it.

For me, the experience was a bit more real and lived. Racist remarks and bullying and degrading behaviour towards me were a daily constant. I didn't know what to do: I had no help or support from anyone, so I put on a brave face. However, I did have five close friends who liked me for who I was, not what I was. Thankfully they are still friends 50 years on.

Because I didn't know what to do, I had to find my way and I found it in books. I found knowledge; I became a sponge, reading literature, geography and science. The bigger the book, the easier I could hide behind it. No one could see me. It was my mask.

Time passed and so did the behaviour. The racism seemed to stop but I remained on high alert. People moved on and we went off to the real world of work. It's hard to believe but perfectly mature adults were still able to resort to some form of bigoted behaviour towards me in later years.

Recently, a rather traumatic court case that lasted three years resulted in the closure of my business. I lost my livelihood and my pension, received a suspended sentence and all this threw my family's lives into chaos. In court it felt like I was back in school; I wasn't allowed to actually defend myself. Someone else was speaking for me while the people prosecuting sat in all their finery: medals and silver were judge and jury.

Here was a different type of bullying, of the official kind. I was looking at a big book that I couldn't hide behind this time. Nothing was said about all the good I did; what I didn't do was the total focus. The day before the final trial and sentencing I actually had a physical breakdown, it all came out. I had no more fight left in me.

I couldn't do it anymore; my mask was ripped out of my hands and I felt naked and exposed.

The comments here are my view and feelings of it and not necessarily the view held by those who brought the prosecution in the first place.

Not long after this a business colleague took his own life.

In all honesty I didn't know him all that well, but when we were together, we shared so many valuable insights. We'd had breakfast together a week or so before he took his life. He was a very positive person and had put into perspective my own ordeal for me.

We talked about books and recommended reading for each other. We talked about personal development too. He was on the cusp of getting the biggest contract of his working life; he'd spent three years working on it. The success of this would launch him globally; he was so excited. I received the phone call of his passing as I was walking into a concert; the floor opened and I fell into it, absolutely stunned.

He had written a letter to be read out to the congregation. Explaining why, what led to it and asking us to forgive, not judge him. I knew only too well the dark place he wrote about. I was introduced to his wife later and she said, "He talked about you all the time." I was floored yet again; I then knew he wore a mask like I did.

After the funeral I sat and reflected on my own. I thought about everything that had gone on and what I'd been through. What was the state of my own mental health? How could I have gone through all this stuff unaffected? The discrimination of being mixed race caused me untold distress growing up, but we weren't supposed to be depressed. It didn't exist, well not from where I was from... I learned to wear a mask.

The stigma from the industry I had been well respected in soon turned on me after the court case. They believe they are right in their opinion, but they've never asked me mine. I left that industry, or it left me. It doesn't matter now; what's done is done.

Five years on I've turned a corner; life is good now. I've come out the other side acknowledging who I am. I am happy and I like *me*. I'm in a different business now, I love it and it's working out to be more lucrative than the one I was in before. I reserve time for two organisations that help the community and I am part of that too. My local community is important, something I had discounted before.

I love to talk to anyone who feels they are being discriminated against or being stigmatised about their feelings, lack of confidence or self-esteem. I show them it's ok to hide behind a mask. It's all about them liking and learning to feel good about themselves, not making others feel good for a quiet life. If that person is you get in touch with me.

I am never alone in my thoughts now and my brave face is gone. The mask I now wear is the real me.

Thank you for reading,

Brian

EMMA-JOEL COKER

Once upon a time there was a little girl named Emma-Joel Coker, who amongst all the madness and chaos of her childhood found an amazing sense of freedom in reading her favourite books. Emma-Joel's dream was to one day become a famous author and pen her own fiction novel based upon her extraordinary upbringing.

That dream has now taken flight. To date, I have spent 30 years working with individuals across the globe to attract and coach talented sales people. I have a holistic approach to enabling and effecting change in my work and that drives me to work in a mind, body and spirited way; creating positive impact in sales professionals' everyday working lives. I spend my day leading a global Sales Effectiveness and Enablement team who are passionate and can drive individuals to achieve personal and professional goals.

I have a first class degree in life and a passion for excellence when it comes to seeing my clients find their wings and soar to the heights they set themselves. Life is too short to not live it in a passionate and compelling fashion because even though a storm may arise there will ultimately be a rainbow.

47 Minutes

I looked at the clock and pronounced the time just like you hear them do in the movies. Time of death 9:51am. I sat there motionless, glued to the spot, but calm for the first time in days.

Nobody prepares you for this moment so you do what you think is best, is expected, or you feel is what any dying person might want. Nobody prepares you for the death of your father and nobody prepares you for the death of your father when you are sitting in bed right next to him.

I closed his eyes, stroked his forehead and sat there staring at the clock. I had given myself 9 minutes before I would call the nurse, I wanted those last precious minutes of just me and him before the process started where he would be in the hands of 'others' or hospital staff as they were really known. Over a period of months and weeks they had become well known to me, but on this occasion they were strangers and I didn't want them anywhere near me for those last few precious minutes.

I don't suppose any child has a plan when their parent dies, but in our heads we sort of know it's going to hurt, we know it's going to come and we do our best not to discuss it, well especially not with 'them'. I sadly am a bit different. I did have a plan, I did sort of know what I would do and we had sort of discussed it.

My father was an alcoholic, there you go, I've said it…God rest his soul! It's taken years for me to say that and even now I can see Dad looking away from me and shaking his head. In fact, I can almost hear him tutting! He wasn't your standard alcoholic, he didn't drink blue cans of Tenants Extra, dress like a tramp or live in squalor.

He was well groomed, his home was his castle and his car was so clean you could literally eat your dinner off it. My father was very hard-working, travelled the globe and was a one-off in his field of work. In fact, just before he passed away he was one of only five people schooled and experienced in a certain make of generator and companies paid a lot of money to contract my father for that knowledge. Hence the reason his tipple was champagne, his favourite meal was lobster and before he died he bought a Bentley, which he proudly drove to the launderette.

We had a troubled relationship. We went months, sometimes years between speaking and seeing each other and at times I wished he wasn't my father. Some people said we were too alike, some people said we looked alike, but for many years all I felt was shame. I felt shame for all the times we argued, for the fear I had and for all the times we missed.

Luckily for me he never gave up and luckily for him neither did I. You see I loved him; I loved him so deeply I thought my heart might burst. When we did get the chance for a hug he held me so tightly I could literally feel all the broken pieces fitting back together and I felt safe. I can remember those hugs as if they were only yesterday.

They said on arrival to A&E that I was a day too early, that they had not got all the tests back yet and could I not come back tomorrow. I was in Bruges, we had come by taxi and my father was literally dying in front of me. The cancer had really taken hold over the last few weeks and his bones were beginning to break, he weighed 54 kilos and he couldn't swallow anymore because the tumours were so large.

The doctor said they suspected TB and I laughed. I didn't mean to laugh, but really could they not just deal with the obvious and stop trying to be so clever. I did my best not to shout and handed them the doctor's note. I didn't speak the language so I had asked my father's doctor to explain why I had hailed a cab from Holland to Brugge. Thankfully the letter did the job.

I whispered in my dad's ear, "They think you have TB." He grinned as if to say 'oh good it's not cancer' and I smiled. He really didn't want to die of something so obvious.

I had always envisaged a phone call, a lady who I hadn't met, but with bright red nails and a hand full of expensive rings calling me to say that he was dead. I imagined a trip to his house where I had never been to collect a load of bin bags, a few pictures and maybe the odd strange item like a sword or a diving knife. I certainly didn't imagine climbing into bed next to him, putting my arms around him and saying goodbye from everyone in my family. I didn't imagine telling him I was going to be great, ok, fine and all would be well as he gasped his last breath and I certainly didn't think it would be one mile up the road from where his parents were killed. I didn't imagine it would take 47 minutes!

At exactly 10am I took a deep breath, untangled my hand from my father's now very cool grip and walked towards the door. It had been chaos on floor 11 of the hospital before my father passed, but now all I could feel was silence, an eerie void, as if the whole world had been put in slow motion.

The attending nurse appeared, took my hand and cried. In fact several nurses appeared, gave me a hug, consoled me in broken English and Dutch and then stood to one side as I was motioned along the corridor to the nurse's station. I glanced behind me one more time to my father's room, I knew what needed to happen next and I was given a 30 minute break whilst they 'laid him to rest' in a hospital fashion and filled out a few forms. I had been asked to select some clothes that I might like him to be dressed in upon my return, but alas I hadn't packed very well.

I hadn't really given much thought to what I might like my father to wear. Dear God he loved clothes and shoes, but today was not going to be his proudest moment of fashion. It troubled me and I began to feel the tears pour down my cheeks. How could something so silly start me off? How could something so meaningless after all that I had experienced in that room bring me to my knees in the hospital canteen? But it did!

I proceeded to let the tears stream down my face and was now void of expression and words. I could feel all eyes upon me as I continued to be amongst 'The Dutch'. You see, I was now all alone, orphaned and in unfamiliar territory with absolutely no clue as to what I should, could or would do next. Who should I call, who really cares and who really wants to know? What the hell do I say? Regrettably my mother and father had parted badly when I was very young, my sister and I had different fathers and I was now divorced. Who in God's name can I tell? 30 seconds later a name appeared in my head.

It was Joery, the son my father never really had, but I knew he meant the world to him. I had only met him once when he was 9, but Joery was now 24 and we were about to meet for the second time and in a very different setting. One where at least he could survive. He was born in Holland, a native, spoke several languages and was about to become the only family member in my life who could even understand or share my pain. I was grateful.

I was asked to return to 'The Room' for one last time to greet my father and to say goodbye. He was now stiff with an odd looking smirk on his face that was a result of his last gasp. I wondered if it was because all I had to dress him in was a t-shirt with a logo of 'The Jam' on it, a pair of blue and white check summer trousers and a cravat. I still to this day think that is exactly what his smirk was about. It helps me to think he might have been smiling behind that exterior pose he now gave.

I felt empty, sick, dazed and in a great amount of indescribable emotional pain. I kissed his forehead, gazed into his beautiful blue eyes and held his hand for the last time.

However, 3 years on I am eternally grateful. I wouldn't have had it any other way and although it hurt like hell and still does, it has been one of my richer experiences. From that moment, nothing in my life has ever been the same and never will be.

My father left me a gift, in fact he left me many gifts, but the one I value the most is his legacy of writing. He wrote pages and I found them all. He loved life, he liked it fast and he liked it hard and now it's my turn to tell our story.

Balls of Joy

My exact words to myself were, "I'd like to give it a go. I have plenty of space, I have time, oodles of love to give and it will be amazing fun."

Give it a go? I don't give anything a go. Let's be honest, I am an all or nothing, sort of girl.

Childless, unemployed, single, in a temporary rented home and ready for adventure. More importantly I wanted to feel again, to love again and to cry again but for all the right reasons.

I had buried myself in work since he'd been gone, worked my backside off and had saved for the first time in my life. So I could re group, look forward, look up and decide on my bright new future.

It was 'Emma Time', 'Team Emma' and time to put me first. I hadn't done that since 1996 when I had a head full of goals, dreams, potential and the chance to achieve all that society expected from a girl like me.

I had become very 'beige' of late and I wasn't happy with the current coasting route of my life's sat nav. I'd lost meaning and purpose. I chose instead to lead a quieter life and one without unnecessary drama, which seemed to be at the core of my existence. 45 years of drama had exhausted me and I wanted to vanquish that gravitational pull it had on my life.

I didn't really have a plan per se but more of a desire, a hunger, a thirst; however looking back now it was just a very annoying itch to love again. To look deep into someone's eyes, say I love you and know they loved me. To plan to wake up next to that person for as long as the universe would allow. My bed had been empty and my heart was a tad sore. My narrow focus did not contemplate nor consider that driving to a small village in the depths of Surrey, would release me to overcoming all of that. But it did.

They say gifts don't always come in the packaging you expect. They were right.

She was sitting on the opposite side of the road. I had seen a picture, been given a little history and a small backstory but nothing prepared me for this. I was handed a tin, a faded green tennis ball and a brown leather lead. "She loves a tennis ball, but she is just too big for our garden" they said and off they went.

She stood up all the way home in the car, yet seemed pretty comfortable. I wondered if, over the last 6 weeks, she had been transported from pillar to post. It's called the lucky hour, the 7th hour of the 7th day and in that last hour before they 'PTS' (put to sleep), they call a few local vets to arrange a slot. This vet thankfully made another call and the right one.

The date was the 23rd October. That was my grandmother's birthday and her name was also Daisy!

"Come on Daisy, let's go and see your new home."

I wasn't prepared at all. 24 hours ago I made a phone call and 24 hours later here I was, a foster mum to a beautiful Daisy Dog. We sat in the kitchen and just looked at each other. What now? Food? A pee? A walk? Instead, we just sat there very contended in not knowing what to do next. So, we did nothing.

I didn't hear her bark for 3 days. Not a peep; voiceless, silent yet she had the most perfect face. I noticed that around her eyes there was this unbelievable heart shaped line of fur; as if it's been drawn and then smudged and shaded to perfectly fit the shape of her face. On her back behind her shoulders were two light brown shadows in her fur that seemed to take the shape of angel wings. I began to believe this wonderful foster dog was indeed heaven sent. Of course she is, she's my grandmother. Sadly, my grandmother and I didn't have quite the picture-perfect relationship so I assumed I might be in for some surprises. For starters, Nan as I called her, had a fascination with choppy waters and stormy seas. Her life was almost as turbulent and when I was 10, she emigrated to Canada to start a new life so I don't think grand parenting was high on her list of priorities.

As I looked at Daisy, I wondered what traits she may have brought back to this life as my new 4-legged daughter. My first 2 months were indeed choppy! Here is the abridged version of life so far:

Week 1: Daisy decided I didn't need anyone else in my life and wouldn't let anyone past the front door.

Week 2: Dog behaviourist training to allow friends and family in to meet my new 4-legged daughter.

Week 3: Emergency vets when raw food diet nearly killed new 4-legged daughter.

Week 4: Call to rescue centre questioning my sanity and wondering how an earth normal mothers handle sick children; well ones that can't speak.

Week 5: Sold fancy two-seater sports car in favour of beaten up old ford escort because 4-legged daughter didn't take too kindly to leather bucket seats.

Week 6: Two minute record for destroying new dog toy and a new Saturday morning routine to search for dog toys that were indestructible.

Week 7: I'm in love and we are now sharing a double bed.

Week 8: 4-legged daughter has her own cupboard, drawer and plethora of outfits - well, it is Christmas!

Week 12: First kennel drop off and 4-legged daughter was having none of it. I cried for an entire hour and nearly broke the speed limit racing back to collect her.

Week 32: She is a dairy free 4-legged daughter (she is not related to my grandmother yippee, Nan ate 4 cream cakes every Saturday without fail). Please don't ask me how I knew; I found out the hard and the very messy way!

Week 75: I cried, I sobbed, I paced and then I lay next to 4-legged daughter on kitchen floor stroking her head whilst announcing in floods of tears, "Don't worry Darling, there are two barren girls in the house now so you are in good company." as she recovered from her doggie hysterectomy.

Week 85: First mother and 4-legged daughter holiday - an expensive cottage that catered for her every need - a bit like paying for public school and the uniform but you don't get a parent's evening or school play.

Week 122: 4-legged daughter is better than an alarm system and who needs a full night sleep when there are foxes to chat to all night every night.

Week 221: 4-legged daughter decided the cat needed chasing but wanted me to come along with her on the end of her lead. The flight over three wheelie bins, three concrete plant pots and along the rather sharp curb gifted me a broken shoulder and three cracked ribs, but I did get to meet all of my new neighbours so that's a positive!

Week 256: Celebrating and preparing for our upcoming relocation to Austin, Texas in 2020…. she really is my grandmother !!

We have had the most amazing adventures together and I often wondered why I had chosen to wait so long to find a love like this. But time is the only real currency when it comes to one's own heart.

Daisy is strong, bossy, funny, clever and loyal. She loves company, once you are allowed past her first bark and the initiation of showing you her selection of balls. She loves a walk in the woods, is a proper water baby, loves being in the car with the wind in her face AND she loves me as I do her.

It turns out there is no 'I' in Team, but there is a 'DOG' in mine and one that has taught me how to be loved again.

Daisy was adopted within one week and this rescue story continues to bring me constant balls of joy.

As with any bouncing back journey there are always bumps in the road and heart wrenching moments. But every day the ball does bounce and it's brought back with a loving smile and a wag of the tail. My 4-legged daughter is, and will continue to be, the love of my life. Who rescued who is something I doubt I will ever be able to answer. Some things are best left unsaid.

KASSI-JAYNE MARSHALL

Kassi is a full time Legal Support Assistant working for a Bristol law firm.

After spending years dealing with bullying by students and teachers alike, in her final school year Kassi could only cope with 2 hours a day and was left with low confidence, depression and anxiety. However, she left education with 9 GCSEs and a college diploma.

Between lacking confidence and unsympathetic employers, when she started work her anxiety flared and this led to unhappy jobs and yet more pressure.

This is where Kassi took her happiness into her own hands; she sought professional help and started her own business. This started a new found love of the business world.

Now in charge of her own future, Kassi is less stressed, learning new skills and flourishing!

Mentioned in this story is Kassi's first business Tenacious PA, which has since closed. However, you can reach Kassi through her new craft shop:

Facebook: www.facebook.com/Stitchfierce

Instagram: @Stitch_Fierce

Triumph

Have you ever been the butt of a joke?

How about shouted at?

How about punched in the back?

Had your hair pulled?

Had someone threaten to push you in the school pond?

Strangled?

Slapped?

I'm sure the list could go on, but my hands already shake when I think about it.

For over 14 years of my life, this was what to expect daily. Before we get into the details, I should start off with saying: I am happy.

My current life is heading down a path that I chose myself, which I worked hard to forge and I am excited to see where it takes me.

I am happy.

So where to start, but the beginning?

In primary school, I had a few close friends and they were my world. I looked forward to going to school each day - I relished in building new relationships and learning new things. We had school assemblies where we'd all sit on the floor, sing songs, listen to the teachers, whisper amongst ourselves and get told off for not listening. I remember talks about how some teachers had received complaints about this thing called 'bullying' and that we should all be nice to one another - and that was that.

After a few months when we were all settling in to the routine and enjoying time with our friends, I got called fat. It was by a boy in my class that had barely spoken a word to me since the first day and all of his friends laughed. So I laughed. "She's so fat, she's as fat as the world". He laughed and pointed at my stomach. I laughed along and walked away, confused by the rude thing he said, but everyone laughed so it must be a joke.

I was happy.

After a few years, I knew the word 'bully' and the jokes were more frequent. I still had some friends and they laughed too, but still, they were laughing so 'it must be a joke'. I sat through lessons, ignoring the boy kicking the back of my chair, or the girl whispering to her friend and pointing at me.

I told my mum the 'funny' joke the boy told at school and she looked at my dad with unsure eyes. She went to my teachers and that Friday morning we had an assembly about 'bullying' and were told to be nice to one another, that was that.

I was happy.

Skip ahead to secondary school. On my first day, Mum took a photo by the gate before I went inside to find my new friends. We were given our timetables and sent off to lessons. On the way down the stairs from my first lesson in a swarm of girls hurrying to their next class, I was punched in the back.

By the time I turned around, there was nobody behind me. I told my friends and we laughed it off as someone ignorant knocking me with their bag, but you know as well as I do that a bag doesn't feel like a fist. I knew there were people worse off than me, so it couldn't be bullying.

I was confused.

Years on, I knew they weren't joking, I knew who my bullies were and I didn't like school any more. I faked headaches and made my voice hoarse so that Mum wouldn't make me go, but she knew I was lying and off I went.

I'd sit in a corner, or bury myself in my small group of friends. I'd pretend it was fine and that I didn't see the face 'she' just pulled at me while the rest of them laughed behind her. I'd also pretend that my so-called friends weren't spreading rumours about me and calling me names. I struggled to find an excuse for the time I asked a girl in my class to let me pass her and she replied with a slap to the face.

I was hiding.

By the final year of school, I had been to counselling. I had been to the school nurse so often she didn't believe me anymore and some of the teachers were as bad as the bullies – or worse because they knew better. I'd spend hours in the evenings crying to my parents about what happened. I didn't do my homework because I was busy being physically sick with worry or shying away in my room, crying and begging Mum not to make me go tomorrow.

Some days Mum would drop me at the gate, watch me inside and then as I watched her drive away, I'd hop into the field next door and walk to meet the friends I made outside of school instead.

I was running.

Eventually though, there comes a day where everybody snaps. My mum snapped when a girl held me over the school pond, threatening to let go and drop me in. Before I knew it, I had run through the gates, down the road and a mile away to cry at my nans' front door.

Mum and I had a meeting with my doctor and the school liaison: my anxiety was affecting my work and health so I would be allowed to school for 2 hours a day. We worked my schedule to fit in the most important lessons and I took the rest of my work home. I had few friends left, but that didn't matter because I would be leaving soon - I wasn't going to sixth form anyway.

One day, I was in my tutor room trying to print off some work and the girls kept turning my computer off. Enough was enough; it was my turn to snap. I threw the computer keyboard at the wall, swore at them to go away and ran out of the room, shaking and crying with anger. I stumbled down the stairs to find the teacher and ask him to let me go home. I explained about the girls and nothing was done.

I was terrified.

Finally, the day came where I'd sat my last exam and the results showed that I had done well enough to go to college to study for a BTEC.

I was ecstatic at the chance to leave behind the horrible jokes, sneers, slaps and punches from my school life. After all, students at college are more grown up than those at school, right?

Wrong.

Queue another 2 years of names, jokes, tears and running away. On two occasions I sat down with my course tutors and told them I was leaving. By now, I had learned that jokes aren't always funny and 'friends' aren't always friends.

I was depressed.

After college came work, more stress, more know-it-all bosses, more misunderstanding and more anxiety. One boss accused me of gross misconduct due to a discrepancy in my timesheet thanks to an incorrect clock in a hallway - something one of the staff later admitted to.

Another said my gastric flu was 'nothing but a hangover' and fired me on the spot (I sarcastically wondered if they would have preferred me vomiting in the restaurant). I didn't even bother giving them the doctor's note I had excluding me from work.

I was exhausted.

One evening after work, I was sat at home talking to Mum, crying (this is starting to sound familiar, isn't it?) about the panic attack I had at work that day, wondering if it was ever going to get better.

I had seen jobs work for other people, so why was it so hard for me?

It was then that Mum suggested I go self-employed. I had done some short-term administrative work in the past and really thrived in that environment. I had watched her set up her own business while my sister and I were at school, so why couldn't I do it too?

The more I thought about it, the more it made sense. I started doing some odd jobs for friends and family and it was like I had found my calling. In early 2014, I picked a name and took the plunge. Tenacious PA was official.

We come to today. I sit here, the proud owner of my own business, working hours that fit the life I am building. I work a few days a week in my Granddad's office and divide the rest between amazing clients, friends and myself. I still struggle with depression and anxiety, but thanks to my family and my real friends I can cope.

I could get upset about the horrible people I dealt with when I was younger. I could point fingers and throw blame until I'm blue in the face, but I am slowly letting go of them. I may never forgive them truly; I don't think I want to. Instead, I choose to thrive. I am learning to love myself for all the things they refused to see.

I choose to pass on my experience with my head held high and hope that others can learn from my story.

I want you to learn to laugh at jokes that are funny, not at your expense.

I want you to learn that just because someone 'has it worse' doesn't mean you can't be upset.

I want you to learn that you are human, real and deserving and no one should have the power to make you feel like you're not.

I want you to learn to love yourself.

I have learned that I deserve better.

I am valid.

I choose to be **happy**.

LAURA BARNETT

Laura is all about Freedom To Live! Running her own businesses since 2007, after 10 unpredictable years in marketing, she sought to do something that would provide her with the freedom and independence she craved and most importantly everyday happiness.

At the heart of Laura's diverse skills is the desire to help people succeed in enjoying life. Through business development, health and wellbeing education and lifestyle coaching she strives to help others design a life to their ideals.

You can reach Laura at:

Twitter: www.twitter.com/freedom_to_live

Life is like a Yo-Yo

"Where's my suitcase?"

Three words that will forever remind me of June 2015. Headed to Marbella for a family celebration, eight of us have just piled out of the taxi at Gatwick. It's 7am. This is where it begins. Instant panic ensues – we check all the luggage on the pavement with Mel, ticking off individual cases, buggies, car seats, and pushchairs! "No, it's not here – the big black suitcase with all the children's clothes, sunscreen, toiletries, and my wardrobe. It's still on the landing."

Quick as a flash her husband Paul makes a decision to call the taxi back, return home, pick it up and meet us all in departures. Into task mode straight away Mel dials the taxi, Paul ferrets in the nappy change bag for his passport and boarding pass and we all agree to get checked-in and ready for the flight, which takes off in just over two and half hours! No problem – the house is only sixty minutes away via the M25! In less than ten minutes taxi man is back and Paul's jumped in and gone, with a wave and parting comment of "See you at the gate, it'll be fine". The rest of us – two couples and Mel, with her two children under four, are gathering various paraphernalia off the pavement and delegating responsibilities including managing a toddler on a Trunki and a crying baby in a pushchair! I don't have a watch, but I know time is of the essence.

Through the airport double doors, chaos and noise hit the senses. We scan the TV screens displaying hundreds of options for flights to destinations all over the world. The trusted orange flashes of Squeezyjet shows itself as zone C, with long waiting lines announcing the designated area for cheap and cheerful, holidaymakers like us. We join the queue and slowly meander our way around the snaking barriers. Time is ticking along, every five minutes there's an urgent shout from a uniformed member of staff clutching a list of flights departing shortly. Debates bubble in the queue assessing the various inefficiencies of the process and the laborious task of simply getting your luggage on-board.

An hour's now slipped by, another two desks open, causing a stir of excitement among the waiting travellers. "It'll be fine," was heard echoing through the hustle and bustle. We reach the front, staying together, checking the cases. Turns out two of us didn't even need to hang about with hand luggage but hey, we're all together and the word from Paul is he's got the suitcase and he's back on the motorway! We tell the uniformed lady of his late arrival – lost passport being the more legitimate excuse put forward. She instructs us to send him to the front desk as soon as he arrives. Great, it'll be fine!

Next stop, security. We get to the designated family access point, allegedly designed to be quicker, but the pace we're going certainly doesn't feel like it. The queue moves painfully slowly, time is ticking along and we finally reach the conveyor. Things are bundled into boxes ready for scanning – shoes, belts, phones, socks, wallets, carry-ons, cosmetics – all laid out on display. I'm first through, no beeps. Next, John my other half; then the parents; and finally the pushchair with Mel, baby Oliver and four year old Oscar. All clear. Phew. But a second look shows most of our bags have been separated for a further security check.

Turns out the iPad should have been removed too. Mum and Dad are unaware of the 100ml liquid rule. Still packed in their hand luggage and also over the maximum limit, mum watches despondently as sun cream, after perfume, after moisturiser gets unceremoniously thrown in the bin. For her, that's about fifty of her hard earned pounds just disregarded. With murmured sounds of agitation, about 1kg lighter and another fifteen minutes later, we're fully clothed and only waiting for the baby food to be checked. All clear, Mel is now sorted, belongings gathered and children strapped in. She's quite calm considering.

Onto the departure lounge. We're looking forward to coffee, breakfast, a pee and perhaps some shopping. Mel's phone chimes with a message, Paul's nearing the M23 junction no more than a few miles away – he's going to make it.

All the while, Oliver's been whiney, but he'll have to wait a bit longer. There's been nothing dramatic with either little one, no tantrums or disasters just a few odd smells, hungry grizzles and typical toddler attention needs. "What's the time?" I ask as we head into the main hubbub. I've already seen the departure board flashing 'last call' on our flight. With the knowledge that our appointed gate is a fair step away and that Mel needs to get nappies changed and bottles of water replaced, I thought a gentle question would be prudent to focus our next steps. Time's running out.

We stride through the frenzy of duty free shopping toward the gates. Luckily, we're not the furthest away. Once there, we notify more orange clad staff that Paul will be here. His name is taken as our passports and boarding passes get checked again and the bus pulls up outside to take us off to the Tarmac. We let everyone else pile on first, we've got excess baggage: pushchairs to collapse, car seats to carry and bags to be re-organised. Since those three little words were uttered just two and a half hours ago, we've not stopped! Mel's phone is just about audible over Oliver and Oscar's constant chattering and the hundreds of people filing past us to the bus. It's Paul.

He's been refused check-in at the front desk.

Too late.

Gate is closing.

If only he hadn't had that suitcase to check-in!

Remarkably, Mel is still calm.

What do we do now? Everything's not fine.

The only option is to go ahead without him. We're the last to board the bus. It takes us ten minutes to reach the aircraft, another ten to board and then another forty, before we actually depart due to a maintenance issue! He could probably have made it in all honesty, but here we are now cruising at 37,000 feet – a man down and not knowing when we'll be reunited! We can't worry from up here, so let's enjoy the fact we can sit down and finally have that coffee and breakfast. I'm wondering what on earth Mel must be feeling at this point. After forgetting the bag, now missing her husband and dealing with the kids single-handedly, I put my head back to contemplate and listen to some tunes. Suddenly, there's a commotion next to me – it's Oliver, he's been sick... all over Mel! She laughs and grabs the wet-wipes.

So what's the point of my story, which forms only the first few hours of a weeklong family holiday? It's that stuff happens. Whether we like it or not, things go wrong. This is an extreme example, I appreciate that. How many challenges do we actually face in any single day? Forgetting the school lunchbox, taking a wrong turn, choosing what to have for dinner, finding the right outfit, juggling deadlines, losing keys, feeling poorly or an unexpected bill. Have you ever sat and really thought about it? If you did, how many of those challenges would you actually just take in your stride, find a solution and move on?

Each and every day we are faced with numerous challenges, some greater and more difficult, exciting or terrifying than others. Each with their own unique and individual impact on day-to-day living. Some short, some long. Some major, some minor. It would be wholly unrealistic of me to suggest that life is perfect – a lot of it is out of our control. But what I can say, categorically, is that where there is Ying, there is Yang. Whatever bad stuff happens there also has to be good.

Just like a yo-yo, when you're in control of it, it rolls down the string and naturally springs back up. And the same is true of life. You're in control of the ups and the downs. You have the power to manage exactly how impactful they are. If you choose not to be in control and to let the yo-yo hang aimlessly on its string, you will struggle to find the momentum to spring it back up.

That's what bounce means to me. It's the knowledge, not only that there is always a positive to a negative, but also that we have innate 'BOUNCEBACKABILITY'. We can deal with anything. It's just that very often we don't even recognise the challenges that we've faced and overcome – let alone give ourselves a pat on the back for it.

Why not take a moment? Look at your day today, or yesterday and really think about the challenges you were presented with, small or large, and how you overcame them. Give yourself some credit where it's due and see that you are in control of your yo-yo. You have the power within you to spring back up whenever you choose to.

And, in case you're wondering...

Paul arrived 4 hours later on another flight. We didn't get the right hire car, got lost on the toll road to the villa and it turned out that Oliver had a tummy bug. Yet, despite all that, we did have a lovely family holiday.

Still Up & Down

Wow, its been five years since that family trip and as usual 'life' has delivered plenty of ups and downs in that time.

Work wise the roles have reversed at home. I opted to take an employed role, so that the other half can pursue his lifelong dream of becoming a qualified professional golf coach and player.

Personally we've had bereavements, cancer scares, surgeries and leaky roofs, as well as amazing holidays, weddings, charity fundraisers and memory-making adventures with family and friends.

Those are the 'biggies' in terms of things affecting our emotional state and wellbeing. We often discount the positives because we feel happy and unaware of their effects, thinking it is the norm, but we can succumb to the negatives when they are obvious life-affecting events. Yet, going back to my story, there are times when smaller, day-to-day issues occur and have effects without us realizing; be it positive or negative.

This is my experience of late. I've been unaware of the effect of daily stresses at work until recently. They have started to physically and mentally manifest in ways I'm not used to, pushing me outside of my comfort zone and testing my resilience.

I know that for the time being, work is serving a purpose and it can only be a negative part of my life if I choose it to be so! I know that by being more self-aware, I am able to adapt my usual self-care routine to manage these new challenges and restore balance. I also know that I'm able to take a step back, get perspective and change my attitude to that of gratitude. However there's a distinct difference between knowing and doing.

So while it's easy to enjoy the ups as they happen, it's essential to have coping mechanisms to minimise the impact of the downs. These three concepts are key to helping me through challenges – they may help you too:

1. Nothing is forever
2. I can and do look after myself
3. Happiness is a daily choice

LAURIE VALLAS

Laurie is a multi-passionate connector, voracious wordsmith and heartist – spotting hearts in everything from floating clouds to a freckled cheek. Curious about practically everything, she loves facilitating the excavation of stories and is drawn to projects that create meaningful legacies. Since participating in *The Missing Piece in Bouncing Back*, Laurie has contributed to several best-selling anthologies and is working on The Heartifacts Publishing.

You can reach Laurie at:

Website: www.theheartifacts.com

LinkedIn: Laurie Vallas

Facebook: The Heartifacts / PositiviTEAs / Laurie Vallas – Author.

Twitter: @TheHeartifacts

Great Expectations

I expected to be a mother one day. Not hoped, not planned – expected. In fact, in my late 20's, I was so confident about this I had offered to donate eggs to a friend who was struggling to conceive. You can imagine when, in my late 30's and nothing had 'happened' yet, I started to become... concerned. In the meantime, I continued to focus on developing my career.

I was stunned the day I landed my dream job, I couldn't believe it! It was in organisational improvement and I was elated beyond expression. A few days later, I paused long enough to realize I was 'late'. When the little blue '+' appeared I felt I had finally landed my 'other' dream job!

I could hardly contain my excitement. I wanted to tell the world and yet the first few days of joy and disbelief were interrupted with moments of concern about 'how could I have both?'

Thinking back, I shudder at how ridiculous I was to even consider these to be parallel achievements.

Then, the day came when the decision was made for me. Four days before Christmas. I felt as though my Soul was pouring out of me and there was nothing I could do to stop it. Nothing.

That was a dark time.

It was dark until I started talking to other women. I was shocked by how common miscarriages are. I am not suggesting that a few conversations fixed everything, but it was certainly a start in my bouncing back.

Months later, my husband and I met with the top fertility doctor in the area. After some tests, it was determined that given my age and uncertain egg quality, I had about a 20-30% IVF success rate. Again, I was disappointed, but undaunted. I began researching for evidence that this was not entirely impossible.

Things were on an upward swing and one random summer Saturday morning my husband asked me, "What if we adopted? What if we adopted a little boy and his sister?" I thought my heart would burst right out of my chest! I never thought he would have been open to that sort of thing. I immediately ran for the computer and registered for the next information session and started to study all I needed to know about the adoption process.

Months passed before I heard anything. Finally I arrived home to a letter from one of the adoption agencies inviting us to an information session. Unfortunately, the date fell when we would be away. I panicked. Immediately, I phoned to see if there would be other sessions – to understand if this would be the only session we were eligible for, etc. This was new to me and I was willing to drop everything to avoid disqualification from this critical step.

The social worker proceeded to ask a series of questions, which I thought was odd, given I was mainly inquiring about future information sessions. However, assuming this was normal protocol, I answered everything. The questions were probing, personal and provocative. When asked if I'd ever miscarried, the pain seized me like it was happening all over again. She pressed on. The momentum was such that there seemed to be no opportunity to halt this slow-moving train-wreck, fast approaching my now-battered heart. I could hardly speak.

Finally, the questioning stopped and she concluded with, "I think it would be best if you contacted an organization called 'More to Life,' as I don't think you or your husband are qualified to adopt…"

I don't remember much after that. It was a Friday, and my husband arrived home to an empty, dehydrated, crushed shell of a being. I was wailing, hard. The noises emitting from me were completely foreign. The miscarriage seemed easier.

I did not move from my bed for five days. The social worker's words pierced my head like nails sealing a coffin. All I could think about was that there may be no more point to my life.

Initially, talking about the experience was excruciating to relive. It took six months to put myself back to some sort of togetherness; a lot of help came from a myriad of therapists, healers and dear girlfriends.

Then, a letter arrived. It was another invitation to an information session.

I began to tremble.

Suddenly I found myself dialing their number.

"Hello, this is X – how can I help?"

"I received an invitation to an information session. I would like to meet with the head of your organization. When are they available?"

"Of course. When would you be available?"

"Right now."

(Startled) "Please hold a moment…The Director would be free at 11am tomorrow. Would that suit?"

"Thank you. Yes, I will be there."

I hung up.

I am not known for my punctuality; however I was sitting in the car park at 10.25am, running scenarios through my mind. What did I want to say? How could I approach this so that the outcome would be of the most value? How could I take this outrageous situation and turn it into something positive for myself, the organization, the children, other prospective and hopeful parents?

The Director had the kindest face and the loveliest of dispositions. She reminded me of both Olivia Newton John and Lindsay Wagner; women I imagined to be approachable and gentle. Lucky for her.

This gave me a stable platform from which to construct a rational conversation. I began by asking her to describe normal protocol for someone phoning to inquire about dates of upcoming information sessions. She asked me to enlighten her of my experience – so I asked:

"Is a full, spontaneous personality assessment of the prospective adoptive mother part of that inquiry about dates?

Is a sight-unseen, speculative assessment and value-judgement about the prospective adoptive father – typical?

Is it usual for the social worker to persist with difficult and deeply sensitive questioning to the point where the caller is in distress – and can no longer speak?

Is it normal protocol to then add, 'You probably need to accept that this process is not for you' – only to rush them off the phone to, presumably, wrap up their day, and go home to their family?

Is it not part of your due-diligence and respect for the human being on the other end of the line – when a conversation has escalated to that level of angst – to not provide a follow-up call to see if they are ok?"

By this time, I was sitting squarely in front of her. Unexpectedly, she appeared to take on my persona – physically curled up as if she were right there on the other end of the phone. She looked helpless; just as I was six months earlier.

She asked if I wanted the social worker to join the meeting. At first, I said no, but then, I felt it was my responsibility to stay the course, follow through with my intended resolution – and leave things better than I found them.

The social worker joined, and before she could say anything, I asked, "Have you ever experienced a miscarriage?" "Yes", she replied.

"How did that feel? Do you remember? Do you remember when that happened? Do you…"

"It was a long time ago," she replied abruptly. "How many women do you speak to in a typical week? Do you even remember speaking to me? Did you ever consider the impact your conversation had on my life? Would it matter to you that I lost five days of my life because of your insensitive and inaccurate assessment of our ability to be good parents? Did you even think about me after you hung up – or was that just another day's work? I wanted to take my own life after that call. Did it ever occur to you how many other women's dreams have been crushed by your callousness? Has anyone ever come back for a discussion like this after a phone call like the one I had with you? Do you ever check the statistics of suicides that may have been related to calls to people like you? By the way, do you have a daughter?"

"Yes – and no, no one has come back…"

"How would you feel if your daughter was treated the way you have treated me?"

Silence.

The Director sat motionless in her chair, weeping quietly.

"I am here because I shudder to think of how many people may have been mistreated by this process. I am here because not everyone has the tools and resources I did to put my shattered heart and broken dreams back together; to pull myself together and come back to look you both in the eye and demand that you not treat couples like this ever again. I am here to put both a face and a voice to all the other women and men who, like me, were totally crushed by your insensitive practice and who did not have it in them to come back to you and demand change. Are you aware of how much effort goes into arriving at a decision like this? To stop trying to make a baby – and to instead, make a life – a family, for parentless children?"

After a long pause and a few sombre conclusions, the shaken social worker excused herself for a meeting. I had clearly made my point.

As the Director walked me to the door, she timidly asked, "Would it be ok to contact you in six months or so, to…?" I stopped her mid-sentence and replied, "No thank you. Please remove us from your mailing list and apologize to the children in your care because unfortunately they will never have the benefit of having been raised by two exceptionally loving people. However I am hopeful that future couples coming to you will now be treated with the individual dignity and respect they deserve and the children in your care will be placed into their loving homes, very soon."

Perhaps I could have been gentler – but that day, the women and men who were turned away before me, were now vindicated. The meeting drew a line in the sand for those that came after me. I have since realised that this very action was what any mother would have done in defence of her children.

I did not have to give birth to awaken my natural maternal instincts. Taking that stand and challenging the status quo was the best gift I could give to those children. I was born to make a difference, and if my purpose is to plant seeds of change that bloom and bear future fruits; then I am a mother after all.

At the time, I never believed I could pull through – never thought I could talk about this experience constructively. I did. I can. I am now able to offer a soft landing for others. Together, we can help each other bounce back!

Great Expectations – Realised

"The final stage of healing is using what happens to you to help other people."
Gloria Steinem

Since the first release of this book, I have come to realise a few things:

- If you want to start a movement – start moving
- If you have something relevant and impactful to share – share something of relevance and impact
- If there is something you can do to help someone – do something to help someone

I would be remiss if I didn't share that when this book reached best seller status, I was stunned. Not only by our collective achievement and that my dream of becoming a published author had begun to become a reality – but the realisation that the almost unapologetic, unbridled account of my grieving experience, combined with an equally unreserved vulnerability that exposed the complexity of my pain and rage – was now available to a global audience.

Upon receiving the book, I read the entire copy cover to cover (my chapter only once) and then thought, "I can't believe I actually penned all that. It's ALL out there now."

Then came, "Oh. My. God. What have I done…? I didn't mean to share THAT much… AND… oh no… people I KNOW are going to READ this!"

Followed by, "Oh no, nooo… now, THEY ALL KNOW!"

I have described the feeling of 'full-on, published emotional nudity' akin to having the entire contents of my innermost secrets downloaded onto a thumb drive and broadcast to every billboard and social media platform for examination, interpretation and, I feared, humiliation.

I am pleased to say all that panic and paranoia was completely and utterly unfounded.

The realisations mentioned above remain a work in progress and as with any journey, I have both good and bad days. As I re-read our stories, I repeatedly remind myself and reassured others; that when it comes to transformation, vulnerability is worth the risk – every time.

***

As with most new experiences, fear can be among the first responses. I find it's helpful to remember that an initial fear of anything is like a passing headache, thirst or hunger; the faster you notice and address it, the quicker it normalizes and rapidly dissipates – often without notice.

Movement requires action.

The most necessary element of sparking meaningful action, is easily ignited through collaboration.

As a child, I remember being told things like, "If you want anything done right, you'll need to do it yourself" and "You can't always rely on other people." The real doozy came in high school when I read Hermann Hesse's, "…no wisdom is better than this when known: that every hard thing is done alone."

Oy. That's a bit of a grim message to absorb during one's formative years. I am so relieved that most of my life's challenges have disproved Hesse's theory.

While the decision to contribute towards, impact and influence broad change was initially individually motivated; in reality, the simple invitation to share my story of resilience in collaboration with others taking the same leap, is how a movement begins and gains momentum.

I remain forever grateful, not only for the invitation, but the gentle, persistent reassuring by both Nicky and our co-authors to keep going and keep sharing.

***

We are familiar with the, 'If you see something, say something' in the context of averting danger. Such framework, constructed out of fear, naturally promotes suspicion. Imagine how conversations could change if we treated this statement as an invitation, and approached the unfamiliar situations with curiosity instead?

The act of extending an invitation of any kind to another is among the most powerful, impactful gestures of kindness we can do for one another. It is an acknowledgement of another's very existence. An invitation not only says, 'I see you', it says, 'You are relevant, and you matter.'

Rather than jumping to a conclusion because someone responds to life (or not) differently than we choose to, imagine what could be possible if we jumped into conversations with compassionate curiosity and asked more questions? When we share experiences and events of personal impact and relevance, the triumphs that have shaped us, we will, and do, impact each other.

Had the conversation with the social worker at the adoption agency taken this approach, it may have had a very, very different outcome.

I make this suggestion because (with full disclosure) it is something I am working on improving. As mentioned earlier, on my good days - I am good at this. On my bad days, the days when I am confronted by my own insecurities and find it difficult to assume positive intent, I need to be reminded that I am not the only one doing the best I can to overcome my wounds and disappointments.

On those bad days, I also need reminders that while it may be hard to believe, anything and everything that has ever been experienced in life by one person, has been experienced by at least one other person (if not hundreds of others) somewhere in the world. No one ever needs to suffer in silence, in shame – or alone. I am tempted to put a stake in the ground and state that there is no such thing as 'alone'.

We may feel it. We may even believe it. But it's just not true.

While I feel that sometimes media can be more 'antisocial' than social, I applaud the positive and helpful ways these macro-platforms have connected people in ways that are truly remarkable – if not miraculous. Let's lean in to the miraculous.

Sharing my story has connected me with the most incredible global network of hearts and minds; creating extraordinary access to a broad and diverse ecosystem of wisdom and perspective. Of the many, profoundly impactful, healing and transformative statements I've heard, one of the more pivotal sound bites is, "…well, there is situational depression and then there is clinical depression. Don't believe everything you assume about your feelings." I'm still searching for an accurate way to describe just how powerful and pivotal this statement was – and continues to be, to me. The words hit me like a meteor. As soon as they landed, it instantaneously both eradicated and evaporated those excruciating six months spent in crippling despair. In an instantaneous split second, I was sucked back into that painful time at warp speed; only to be catapulted back to the present – completely liberated.

Had I succumbed to my imaginary fears, my unfounded shame and not continued to share my story – even what I had thought was an irrelevant excerpt, of how I (*umm…thought I had completely*) bounced back, I may not have ever known there was even more pieces missing, keeping me from experiencing even more peace.

***

I now understand that the journey of both writing and sharing my bounce-back story had everything to do with my own healing and, to be honest, was initially not entirely motivated by the desire to help others. In fact, I am embarrassed to say that I hadn't considered the impact that sharing our experience might have had on my husband.

Truth be told, I didn't write it with an audience of men in mind. Not at all. Which in hindsight, was odd. And of course, life has a way of surprising us. Just when we feel as though, 'Ok – that's done and dusted and I can tick that box off as complete'; we are given more opportunities to keep going, keep learning and keep contributing. Our job is not done when we've healed a wound. Once we've healed, likely with help from others, our responsibility is to help others heal.

A few years ago, a work colleague and friend confided that he was a bit distracted at work because he and his wife had miscarried and that things were understandably difficult at home. He was suffering from this terrible loss on his own, in his own way and had been trying to reach out to his wife to console her and try to grieve together. As time went on, things weren't improving; she had become more withdrawn and he became very concerned about her overall wellbeing.

While I had not met his wife, I immediately felt an instant impulse to reach out and offer support and an empathetic ear. Without ever mentioning that I had also experienced a miscarriage, I brought in a copy of our book and suggested that he give it to her when he felt the time was right.

You can imagine my surprise when he approached me a week or so later and shared that HE had read my chapter and expressed how grateful he was that I was both so candid and vulnerable – because it helped provide perspective and insight into how miscarriage can occur to women. He added that some of the things I had shared, articulated and illustrated how she may be feeling. He went on to say that, "Had you not written this book with such honesty, I wouldn't have known how to approach my wife – and for that, I am truly grateful."

***

I have been asked why we stopped pursuing adoption and there have been times when I asked my heart that question. Every now and again, I'd have a moment – a millisecond of a moment – where I wished we had pressed on.

Actually, we did.

I remember the day when I received a text from my sister – followed by a photo – telling me that she knew of a family of seven boys who would need homes. My husband and I dropped everything and immediately ran out to meet them. After a bit of a journey and only a few months of waiting, we do have a little boy and, unexpectedly, a little girl: Wilson and Fiona. These two are by far the most loved and cherished fur-babies and I am proud to say that they are, fortunately, being raised by two exceptionally loving people. We have been blessed with their unconditional love and affection in a way we had never imagined or experienced. The question is both appropriate and accurate; "Who rescued whom".

It wasn't how we had initially expected our family would come to be, but it's been amazing (to say the least) – and even better and more fulfilling than we could have ever expected – or realised.

It's funny how prayers are answered…

LYNN JONES

Like many others, Lynn slipped the net as a person with Asperger's which lead to the incredible life story she now shares in her writing. Lynn is a woman of courage, who inspires others and campaigns for change through awareness. Her suffering has led to a wealth of understanding on the nature of abuse and the healing power of love.

Through self-directed learning, Lynn works to promote a better and safer way of working for medical students. Through writing and speaking, Lynn works to reduce abuse, promote love and empower people to redress the balance of power. Lynn qualified with distinction at The Coaching Academy as a life coach, helping personal growth and change. She also qualified with the Institute of Supervisory Management and Toastmasters International.

In writing Through the Asperger Window Lynn hopes to give a unique and alternative view of life that challenges the status quo to create better partnerships working between Experts by Experience and professional workers.

Lynn is available for talks and can be contacted on the links below.

Email: jones_m_lynn@hotmail.com

Website: www.lynnmjones.co.uk

Facebook: http://www.facebook.com/LynnJonesAuthor

Warning – Doctors can Seriously Damage Your Health

At the age of 67, I feel happier than I have ever felt in my life. As my husband and I sat in the sun watching our baby grandson playing, it seemed impossible to feel any better than I felt at that moment. No exotic place in the world or personal achievement could top the bliss from this simple pleasure. It is amazing to think that after enduring the agony of emptiness, loneliness, and despair, I could be living with this level of love, joy, and fulfillment. The incredible thing is that on an almost daily basis I now notice some small change within myself that greatly enriches my life.

In 1976, at the age of 28, I started my second pregnancy. A fear started to rise. After the first birth I was anxious about having stitches out, so to help the head nurse provided gas and air that she didn't switch on and took the stitches out with no sedation. This escalated my fear for the second birth and I set out to get reassurance by mentioning it at the first anti-natal visit. The GP was a young locum, who said it would be no problem to give me soluble stitches after the birth if they were needed.

The locum became a partner in the practice and attended the birth, so I felt I would get the care I deserved. He went back on his word and for the second time I was deceived. Not only by the GP, but also the nursing staff who once more went through pretence by giving me a Valium injection they said wasn't working, with more gas and air that was not connected, manhandling me into position to take the stitches out, despite my objections.

I had an emotional collapse and cried to the point of exhaustion from the shock, falling into a deep sleep, where nursing staff took over my baby's next two feeds. If things were not bad enough, when I got home I bled and was distraught at the thought of more problems. Needing support from my husband, I turned to him only to suffer more feelings of betrayed trust when he denied paternity for no reason.

My husband's behaviour left me heartbroken, with feelings of loneliness, emptiness, and despair. Lost and confused, I suffered further indignities of stigma and shame as a divorcee, after breaking up with my husband to remove myself from emotional agony and suicidal feelings.

As a result of the intrusive medical experience, I suffered Post Traumatic Stress Disorder and was left traumatised. I had repressed the cause within my subconscious awareness, and the medical profession saw me as irrational and neurotic when I had a nervous breakdown, yet I was in touch with reality.

Life was hard with no money or car. My baby boys gave me motivation to hold up in life and a reason to live. Considering the pain and weight of the emotional baggage, I did well to survive as a lone parent. My mother and father were supportive, travelling across town twice a week with a food parcel to visit and help.

In 1982, I met Geoff and we married in 1983. The important thing for Geoff and I was family. It was wonderful for both of us to be a family unit.

A month before getting married, I started a supervisory job, setting up a community aid team to visit elderly and housebound people, while giving long-term unemployed up to a year's work opportunity. Starting with just a note pad and pen, I found my natural intelligence, liaising with social and other services to fill gaps, provide a worthy care service, and a high number of staff found employment within the year.

I was promoted to Senior Supervisor and my team expanded from 12 to 60 people, providing a service described as, 'As professional as possible for a non-professional group'. From my experience, I had set up a visionary approach to care.

After four years, rumours went round that management was creaming thousands of pounds from the community programme. I developed an obsession to understand what was happening, as I had put my heart into this work, using it as compensation for the heart-breaking belief I had let my family and babies down by not holding up.

With my thoughts going at high speed and no sleep, I suffered the first of three episodes of psychosis, which meant a new breakdown where I lost touch with reality.

It was after the second psychotic episode that I realised my great fear and breakdown was because I had been sexually abused in childhood, which meant that when the doctor put me through the phobia, I re-experienced the trauma of sexual abuse at the emotional age it happened, with no understanding of the cause or my distressed reactions. With sex as a an expression of love and all that is creative on the one hand and all that can cause abuse and destruction to people's lives on the other, I set out to understand the duality of love and abuse.

My early interests in commerce changed to interest in people and social studies. I attended low brow psychology and sociology events with local education groups. After reading the first page of an 'O' level sociology book, I had no understanding of what was written. From there, I attended classes and read a vast number of pop (popular) psychology books where I noticed a spiritual theme running through many of them.

Motivational CDs have made an incredible difference to my self-development. My life journey might be described as 'From the pits to the Ritz', where wisdom teachings touched me at the depths of suffering, are with me now, and will continue as part of being a life-long learner.

One line quotes have for many years had a profound effect on me, most memorably, 'If you do what you have always done, you will get what you always got'. With sexual and emotional abuse in my background, change was very important to me. Another significant quote was, 'If you want to change the world, change yourself, as everything changes relative'. This has proved very true for me and my world is totally different.

The thing that goes with change is that we lose relationships. One example is when people give up drugs they spend less time with others who take drugs, which is positive. The difficulty comes when the people we need to lose are the ones we love and are significant in our lives. It is then we realise the truth of the saying, 'If we can't say no in the family, we have to say no to the family'.

So, what am I doing now?

Educationally, I am self-taught, having meandered through the fields of social science, using integrity as my yard stick, while I tested truths within the study on myself. I joined The Coaching Academy to become a life coach and after being frozen with fear at the written test, was thrilled to pass with a distinction, which helped to contradict the negative messages of the past from my family that I was 'dim and stupid.'

I joined Toast Masters International and fast tracked through to gain Competent Communicator. With competence in speaking, I approached a local university to talk to students. An opening became available and I gave talks on the importance of therapeutic relationships using client centred approach and client perspective in mental health.

I am able to give students a meditation to show what psychosis was to me with insight into the experience of living with psychosis. I was especially pleased to work with student doctors on the subject of Asperger's and how to identify it in others who have been misunderstood, misjudged, mistreated and, like me, have slipped the net.

Having studied the depths of human nature for 38 years, I have a vast store of knowledge. From the books in the university library, I now realise that what we learn from outside of self is belief, but what we experience for ourselves is knowledge. Another expression that has meaning for me is: 'What got me to this point will not get me to where I need to go'. Progress is about entering new leagues and new dimensions that bring us up against faulty beliefs to break them down and to face fears to overcome so that the potentiality we are born with may flower.

The most momentous thing I have learned about myself is that I am not the person my family and society cast me as. As the youngest female in a working class family, it was my place to be last and certainly not to outshine people with a position of significance. It was not my place to think or to question, but to go along with those bestowed with power and position to make decisions.

For many years my work has been fuelled by belief in what I was doing and the need to right some terrible wrongs from the past. It is the emergence of self-belief that has freed me to move out from an oppressive rank and file way of life, to speak out and show others that with self-belief it is amazing what can be accomplished.

Pilgrim's Progress

Three years have passed since writing "Warning – Doctors Can Seriously Damage Your Health". On a daily basis progress takes place but is hardly noticeable. Now that I stop and look back to that chapter of my life, I can see incredible progress.

I was extremely nervous entering the world of writing, but since then I have written another chapter for a book compilation entitled, "From Brokenness to Wholeness," and in 2019 my first book was published: "Trailblazing the Way From Victim to Victor – Through the Asperger Window."

There were several reasons for writing the book. Since the medical incident that collapsed my life and health, I was desperate to have a voice to speak up and stand up for myself. I needed to be heard in order to right the wrongs of a gross injustice. My journey of recovery has been a painful but therapeutic process to heal and move beyond the trauma suffered at the hands of the medical profession.

Suffering leads to understanding and sharing the learning for the benefit of others has enabled me to reclaim life purpose and bring meaning back into my life.

I was an ordinary person, living an ordinary life for a woman born in 1948, whereby I grew up, got married and had children. From there the medical incident took my life on a downward spiral to the dark night of the soul. All areas of my life collapsed, including family. One of the most painful and darkest moments of my life was when I suffered betrayal from my father and sister, which was emotional agony.

A major part of my journey of understanding was learning at the age of 60 that I had Asperger's, which is on the autistic spectrum. It was a turning point for me, which felt like pieces of a puzzle coming together and life's unanswered questions started to get answers. Life started to make better sense.

One of the biggest differences was that I moved from a need to be understood to understanding many things for myself, including the lack of tolerance people have for one another where there is difference and how cruel people can be. I became obsessed with a quest to understand the duality of love and abuse that exists within human nature.

There are many interesting facts about living with Asperger's. It has helped me to know that people with Asperger's have problems with feelings and can't deal with them at gut level as the average person does. I have to bring everything through the intellect, which means taking everything round and round in my mind to reach a point of seeing. It is exhausting. The average person sees at an instinctive level and has less need to think about things. From a strong sense of feeling I shift to a sense of seeing, which then progresses to a sense of knowing. The cycle is ongoing.

People with Asperger's look out of a different window to the rest of the world. We take in information differently, interpret it differently and come up with different conclusions. Difference is not wrong, it is just different. Asperger perspective gives a whole new view of the world and where would we be without the insights of Albert Einstein or Sir Isaac Newton?

Psychosis was an incredible aid to learning for me. I not only wrote a chapter in my book sharing my experience and findings on psychosis, but I have also lectured on the subject. Going to the far reaches of my mind is something I would most certainly not want to do again. After 3 psychotic episodes life could never be the same again for me. It was like outgrowing the ages and stages of childhood, where regression back to early developmental ways of life is just not possible. I broke through the limitations of mind to witness the terrifying duality of vastness and wonder of cosmic consciousness within psychosis, which I see as spiritual emergence.

Spirituality has been another major factor in my progress. I used to be a devoted church goer, but as a spiritual person with the literalness that goes with Asperger's, I did not fit in and was marginalised to the point that I left the church. It was difficult to leave the church because the word within the message was a lifeline for healing and unity, as it spoke to me about love and living in love and harmony with one another. The hypocrisy from the church was distressing because the word given out and the deed did not match.

Since then I have found my tribe with other spiritual people and am so much happier with those who are on my wavelength. I can see that to the world spirituality is mad and to spiritual people the ways of the world are equally mad. To me, the move towards deeper levels of spirituality is like going from man-made to what is natural. From there I am finding my tribe with people the church would reject. My new tribe has been for me like the Good Samaritan, a group of people where I found healing. From there my intuition is developing and the quality of my inner world is becoming enriched.

My belief system about myself, the world and my place in it felt like the house built on sand, which is a famous parable in the Bible. When the storms of life hit, my belief system did not hold up. My new belief system is more rock-like and while I still hold to the ideal of how spirituality can transform the quality of life for self and others, I now have a more balanced understanding of the realities within the negative side of human nature.

A significant part of living with Asperger's is that I have not been able to see the harm in people. Reality has been a huge shock and rude awakening as my illusory way of perceiving the world broke down.

My move to understanding has been a very long process, starting with victim mentality and the question, "Why did this happen to me?" This led into reading self-help books that were easy reads as pop psychology. From there I progressed to reading O-Level sociology books, ultimately moving on to academic books from the university library. In addition, I have listened to audio sets for personal development for a great number of years. My long journey of progress and change has resulted in transformation.

In my quest to understand the nature of abuse within humanity, a friend directed me to what is generally dismissed as conspiracy theories. It was quite an eye opener. Further to this, I was given a sociology book by a German sociologist which showed that people have hidden agendas to have power and control over others, which would validate some of the conspiracy theories that appear too mad to be true. People with Asperger's don't have or understand hidden agendas, which results in us being gullible and vulnerable adults.

As a person who works to eliminate abuse through exposure and promote the healing power of love, I ask the question, "Why have care, compassion, ethics and all that would contribute to peace been downplayed, while corruption and abuse from world leaders give more power to the domination system and take humanity towards extinction?"

Looking back over my 71 years I have seen care and compassion get pushed further to the margins of life. To me, I have wondered how the spirit of love, relative to care and compassion, is being eliminated. My thought goes to the time horses roamed free. They were considered wild and man set out to tame them. Taming horses was achieved by breaking their spirit. I believe breaking the spirit is what happened to humanity when Native Americans were hounded and witch-hunts happened to create conformity and bring about a patriarchal system of control. From my own experience of spiritual development and knowing others, people who are free do not cause mayhem, but are peaceable people and many become healers. Authorities took the monopoly and became the fount of all knowledge as a visible and significant factor within social control.

In balance with the descent of goodness in the world, I see the ascent of immoral behaviour. My studies have led me to belief it is due to Freud and the emergence of Psychiatry. One four-part series, that has now been removed from the web, stated that Freud plumbed the depths of mind to find that the subconscious was so awful it had to be contained. He shared his discoveries with his nephew, who put the findings into advertising by bypassing mind and conscience and connecting directly with the drives. This is when adverts became sexualised and I believe the full force of the seven deadly sins was released onto the world.

We are each born into the world with unique potential, but lose touch with this as we are crafted by the world to play a role with a given society's social order. How many people can answer the questions, "Who am I, why am I here and what is my life purpose?" One quote that often comes into my mind is from Søren Kierkegaard, "Truth is not because something is added, but because something is taken away." As false beliefs fall away it is not about finding the illusive truth absolute, but finding what runs true to the heart of who we are and I believe this is where humanity will find unity.

My first book was "Trailblazing the Way from Victim to Victor – Through the Asperger Window." The tagline is because my view of the world has Asperger perspective. It exposes abuses that are happening in the world and attempts to show better ways. There is the possibility of another book, which would be on the theme of "searching for the key of life". This would be a more direct challenge to abusive powers, that attempts to get to the heart of the matter regarding love and abuse, which will enable people to see and discern for themselves and allow each of us to make informed choices.

For 43 years I have sought truth and healing following emotional and mental chaos caused by medical abuse. Both quests have reached completion together. I have heard that at the root of all counselling is the relationship with self. This has proved true for me. My breakdown was a spiritual emergency, where I described the pain as dislocation of the soul. I can now see that what got fractured was the relationship with myself. I could not live with the big lie that has been upheld through the medical profession or the shame and stigma of breaking down.

I fully understand my trigger for psychosis and have explained everything fully to the medical profession. They hold on to the diagnosis of PSYCHOSIS in size 72 font, but I can no longer play their game. Ultimately, healing did not depend on them removing oppression, but on me releasing from the fear within internalised oppression. I can now relate to Wayne Dyer when he said, "Your opinion of me is none of my business." Truth has given me a great sense of inner peace, healing and unity as my relationship with self is restored.

MARK BRIMSON

Mark is based in Bristol, UK. He is a Radio Presenter on Duggystone Radio and loves nothing more than getting lost in his music.

He is the proud owner of a 6 year old daughter, Niamh, who makes him laugh every single day.

Sadly widowed at the age of 31, Mark has battled himself back with the help and support of his immediate family and friends.

Mark would like to dedicate his chapter of the book to the army of heroes who helped him achieve what he set out to do in 2017

Websites: www.duggystoneradio.com and www.headwaybristol.org.uk

Gloria

She was working as a waitress in a Bowling Alley when I first met her, not as catchy as the song, but a true story none the less.

It was 1995 and I was on a jolly boys holiday to Jersey with 3 of my friends, when one evening we decided we would go to the Jersey Bowl for a bite to eat! We sat at our table and were served by this amazing dose of Irish happiness. Her name was Gloria and for the next few hours she transformed my world.

Fast-forward a month and we got together. At this point in my life I was living in my home town of Bristol and flying over once a month, then every 3 weeks, every 2 weeks and before I knew what was happening I was going every weekend to see her, so we made the decision that I should simply move there to protect the ozone and my wallet.

Life stayed that way until we decided that we should look to get our own place together and therefore move back to Bristol where I was fortunate to get my old job back again. We married in 2000 in her hometown of Killybegs in Co Donegal Ireland and life was great, we enjoyed our DINK (Double Income No Kids) lifestyle and loved to travel together.

On one of our trips to Australia, Gloria started to complain about having headaches, but we just put that down to overexertion and the fact that we had just spent a heavy evening in Sydney celebrating New Year's Eve in style. A few days later though the headaches persisted, so we decided to get these checked out. At Sydney Hospital and to our relief they too thought she had overdone it with all the flying and late nights we had been having up until that point, so we left there with nothing other than some hydrating tablets for her to take.

6 weeks later back in England again the headaches persisted and by now I was getting more and more concerned about it, so she headed for our local GP who was as much use as a chocolate teapot and simply told her to keep taking the aspirin and "You'll probably be ok!!"

That was my final straw and we decided that we would go down the route of private healthcare and pay for an MRI scan ourselves so at least we could put to bed any worries that it could be anything too serious.

The MRI scan came and went and then the big day arrived when we sat in the consultant's office for him to tell us that we had been worrying about nothing and go back to your lives and plan your next holiday!

Unfortunately that wasn't what he told us, to be honest looking back now that meeting was all a bit of a blur and all I really remember was that the hospital consultant would be in touch soon to discuss the options. What he had actually said I later found out was that, although he didn't think there was anything to worry about, there was a cluster of abnormal blood vessels on her brain, which is known as an AVM (Arteriovenous Malformation).

At that time life was a bit of a daze as we met consultant after consultant and each one gave their own take on what should or shouldn't happen, but then we found a guy by the name of Dr Porter who was luckily based in Bristol and seemed to really know his stuff.

One of the first things I learned about an AVM was that it was a condition that you are born with and that the chance of something unpleasant happening increases by 2% a year. In real terms, this meant that by the time Gloria was 50 she was guaranteed a Brain Haemorrhage or worse. We were given 4 options to consider:

Do nothing, which in all honestly wasn't really an option.

Have Radiotherapy on the affected area, then wait for 2 years to see if it had worked, again not really much of an option.

Embolization, which effectively meant gluing down the affected area until it was a nice hard mass and therefore stopping the potential bleed on the brain – then a year's wait to see results.

Have full on brain surgery cutting out the affected area.

We spent about a year researching, talking to doctors all over the country and eventually decided to go down the route of brain surgery as we felt we really didn't want her to go through a procedure then have to wait a minimum of a year to see if it would be ok. Dr Porter had decided he wanted to do the embolization too so when he did the surgery it should be easier to cut out the mass.

Two weeks before the main surgery she had the embolization done and all went well and on June 5th 2007 Gloria underwent a 13 hour operation on her brain to get the rest out. This was by a million miles the longest day of my life, I just didn't know what to do with myself.

That night Dr Porter called me and his words went like this: "Mr. Brimson, things haven't gone exactly according to plan." Now I was out of my mind with worry, basically what had happened was she had a bleed during the operation which had complicated everything. The next day, I went in to see her and although groggy she was able to recognise me, knew where she was, what day it was and she even knew that I was late! Everything was good there. That evening things were exactly the same and she was stabilizing; everyone was happy.

The next morning at 4am, my phone rang and that is never good news. It had transpired that during the night Gloria had suffered a huge heart attack that she was never to recover from.

So that was me, 32 years of age, widowed and without my soul mate!

There was no book on what I was supposed to do next, although everyone went out of their way to tell me how I should be feeling and what I should do next. In fact the only real piece of good advice I got was from my dad, who told me to make no decisions for a year! The reason I know that it's good advice is because I ignored it.

After taking Gloria home to Ireland to her final resting place (a decision that she would 100% of wanted, but one that has haunted me ever since), I found it really hard to be in the house. Every time I walked through the door I saw her standing in the kitchen cooking, so I decided I would change the house. I put in a kitchen diner and put wood flooring throughout the house 'because it all needed doing'.

The reality of course was it didn't need doing at all and after I finished doing the whole house - guess what I still saw her standing there!

I eventually sold the house - another decision I shouldn't have made. I made lots of bad calls at this time; one of the worst was deciding that I wanted a weekend retreat in Spain. I flew over with a friend, put £6k down as a deposit then came home, promptly changed my mind and lost the money. You can see now why I now know that Dad's advice was good. I was in a really tough spot, huge bouts of depression coupled with really not wanting to live anymore; I simply couldn't see the point in living.

To try to change things, I decided after buying a cricket magazine that I would go to New Zealand to watch England play on a tour. It was here that I vividly remember being in the Bay of Islands sitting on beach with a volcano to my right, golden sand and the bluest sea I had ever seen in front of me. It was in that moment that I decided that life was worth living after all. What better way to honour Gloria's life than to carry on and try to do the things she didn't manage to.

I tried all sorts when I was home to try to get myself sorted. I tried counselling that didn't work for me at all…I felt like I was counselling the counsellor. I was prepared to try anything at this point and when somebody suggested Reiki, I didn't even know what it was. This however had the desired effect on me, I don't understand it and to be honest I don't want to. I just know now that it works and more importantly I know when I need it next, it really helps me to get my mind back in touch with the rest of me.

Life has moved on considerably in the 8 years since Gloria died. At the time of writing, I am a Sales Director for a Merchant Services company and we specialise in helping businesses save money on getting paid.

In 2013, my beautiful daughter Niamh Lilly was born. I cannot express enough how that young lady has made a difference to my life; she has brought a calming influence that I hope that she will never understand.

One last thing I have learned along the way whilst the pain of Gloria's death remains with me: you can do nothing about what went on yesterday, but you can make a huge difference to what happens tomorrow. Oh and listen to your dad - they may be old and doddery, but they have your best interests at heart!

Walk for Glo

The events of that day in 2007 seem so long ago now, but in some ways it still feels like it was only yesterday that Gloria left this mortal world and travelled over to the perceived "other side". In the years that followed I was just existing day-to-day. I was not really achieving anything and if I'm honest I was only just getting by, doing the bare minimum I could get away with to survive another day. I knew that this life wasn't sustainable.

June 7th 2016 was the 9th anniversary of Glo's passing. Sat outside Nando's, having just ordered my takeaway for my tea, I was in absolute bits. I missed Glo like mad. I was in a relationship that made me incredibly unhappy despite the fact that it had produced Niamh, the most amazing daughter anyone could ever wish for. Everything was just getting too much; I knew that if I didn't take control of the situation then I was going to join Glo in the cemetery in Killybegs in County Donegal. So, I did what everyone seems to do now - I recorded a video and posted it on social media. I needed something that was going to hold me to account.

The next day I decided that if I was going to alter my mindset then I needed a positive focus. I set up The Gloria Brimson Foundation with the aim of raising as much money as I could for my chosen charity - Headway Bristol. Soon after this I was on a short break in Spain when I broke the news about the Foundation to my friends Olly Culverhouse and Nick Elston. A few eyebrows were raised when I announced that I intended to raise £10,000 for the charity and if I'm honest I had no idea how that was going to be achieved.

People are incredible and really generous. I found this out soon after announcing the Foundation, when I received lots of offers of help to run, cycle, bake cakes - even schools offered to raise money for me. DJ's offered to put on party nights… you name it, they did it! It was incredibly humbling but I knew that I needed to do something myself, but what?

I was working as a travelling sales manager at that point and spent a large amount of time in my car and that's where I did a lot of my thinking. What could I do to really challenge myself both mentally and physically because, let's face it, I wasn't going to raise that kind of money by putting on a jumble sale! Could I run a marathon? Nope! Was I any good at cycling?

Nope! Could I walk a marathon? Probably... But given the right set of circumstances and the right weather I think anyone could walk a marathon. Could I walk a marathon a day for 5 days straight? That felt like the challenge that I was looking for.

So, the Walk for Glo was born. 5 marathons in 5 days, so who would join me? My first port of call was to ask Nick and Olly if they fancied getting involved and the answer was a resounding yes. Then Nicky Marshall was in and Adrian "Chevvy" Chase soon followed. Paul "Simmo" Simpson, a Bristol Rovers fan I had met on a drunken away trip to Dover a few years earlier, was next to say yes and Mathew "Drive" Poole completed the walking team.

Now for the route. I spent a bit of time deciding the route but the football fan in me quickly took over proceedings. I remembered that the first ever away match I took Glo to was an away game at Plymouth Argyle to watch my beloved Bristol Rovers (we probably lost). It worked out that the route would take 5 days of marathons, at 26.2 miles per day, to get back to The Memorial Stadium in Bristol - so that was sorted.

A few weeks later I was having a coffee with my good friend Laura Barnett and she asked how we were going to achieve the walk. My reply that we were going to drive to Plymouth and simply walk home didn't exactly meet with an approving look and she volunteered herself as the project manager for the trip. Looking back, the work undertaken by Laura was incredible. Booking accommodation, liaising with the Councils, advising police what we were doing etc. Without her none of that would have happened as I had completely ignored the potential for that to be required.

The date of the walk had been set for the following March and with Laura on board all we had to do as walkers was go about our training. We had to build up our stamina to the required distance over a period of time. Unfortunately, Nick didn't think that way and went from walking 5 miles as his first walk to 18 the next week and promptly injured his foot and he was potentially out of the walk! Nightmare!!

The WhatsApp group we set up became busy as we all did our bit and updated the group via Map My Walk. We were willing each other on with every training walk we completed.

Whilst all of this was going on, we had started to get the attention of the local press. The Evening Post, BBC Radio Bristol and The Western Daily Press all covered the story on the build up to the event and we had raised around £2,000 before we had even arrived in Plymouth. We had made an amazing start towards the target amount.

We arrived in Plymouth on the night of 19th March 2017, checked into our hotel and we sat chatting after dinner. I gave everyone an option to get out of doing it, "Look guys, nobody really knows whether we are going to do this thing or not. We could hang around Plymouth for a couple of days, have a spa or whatever." Every member of the team wanted to carry on regardless.

The support crew was immense. Helping Laura was my Dad, "Big Al". He was the driver of the van, affectionately called The Battle Bus, which was stocked with supplies for us all should we need them. Also on the team was Kassi Marshall who was a goddess at running errands during the walk: buying sandwiches or whatever Laura needed her to do next. Sharon Critchlow was our Devon expert – who was to rescue us from a dual carriageway! Nick was effectively out of the walk due to his injured foot, but was inspirational behind the camera as we streamed videos all over social media in the build up and during the event itself.

The route we were taking was:

- Plymouth Argyle FC – Ashburton
- Ashburton – Tiverton
- Tiverton – Taunton
- Taunton – Wells
- Wells – Bristol Rovers FC

We set off on the morning of the 20th March 2017. Drive had been elected as map reader for Day 1 and was armed with everything he needed including instructions from Big Al about which of the 3 roads out of Plymouth we could take. You guessed it - we got lost immediately and practically walked half a marathon within Plymouth itself! The rest of the day was good, the weather not so as it lashed it down for a good portion of the day, but everyone was in great spirits.

Nick did parts of the route but had to be held back from doing more by the rest of us due to his foot. I remember getting to 20 miles and Simmo and I were high fiving like we had done it. I guess in footballing terms we had just scored and we were running around with our shirts off, then we hit the wall. I can promise you the last 5 miles were horrendous and you really had to drag yourself through it. I got to the hotel and was walking like someone who had soiled themselves. I had blisters everywhere and wondered how we could continue to do this, but this team was incredible.

The weather continued to be horrific. The hail storms were especially fun, the wind caused us many issues and the route was every bit as hilly as I feared it might be. But through it all this team kept going and going. Olly and Drive in particular were like a couple of machines leading the group on. Olly had established himself as the group leader from the walkers' perspective. He assumed the role of map reader (Drive having had his map reading contract terminated in Plymouth!) and lead us all from check point to check point, carefully chosen by Laura. As we approached each checkpoint, seeing the bright yellow Battle Bus in front of us was a joy for us all.

Getting to flatter ground and into Taunton on the Wednesday night was a highlight; we started to recognise certain places on the route and you could tell home was in sight.

After a wet day on the Thursday, a lovely sunny greeting awaited us in Bristol with family and friends who came to walk the last mile with us up Gloucester Road.

We raised £10,000 that week alone; largely down to Nick and his social media skills. Literally every time he put out a live video my phone would go nuts and approximately £500 came in. It was an absolutely incredible feat by a very special group of people.

The Foundation ran until the June of that year and we signed off with a Dinner Dance. We eventually raised a staggering amount of money for Headway Bristol: £35,000!

My favourite historical figure, Major Dick Winters of Band of Brothers, was once asked by his grandson if he was a hero. "No, Son" he replied, "but I served with a company of them." That is exactly how I felt about every single person that involved themselves with us on that magical week.

My worst life experience has been turned into my greatest – that's special.

NICKY MARSHALL

Nicky is an award winning, international speaker and best-selling author. She is also a mum, nan and wife and loves nothing more than family time.

At 40, Nicky suffered and recovered from a disabling stroke - inspiring a life's mission to make a bigger difference.

Nicky has an accountancy background and twenty years of helping people improve their health and wellbeing under her belt. Combining both, Nicky is a mentor, seasoned workplace facilitator and keynote speaker, inspiring people to discover their own brand of Bounce! Nicky's knowledge, knack for stress busting, hugs and infectious laugh make her an in demand and popular speaker.

With passion in buckets and a penchant for keeping it simple, Nicky has a unique talent in breaking down the barriers that hold people back from living a life they love.

Be careful if you stand too close - her enthusiasm rubs off!

Follow these links to connect with Nicky:

Website: www.discoveryourbounce.com
Facebook: www.facebook.com/discoveryourbounce
Twitter: www.twitter.com/_nickymarshall
www.twitter.com/dyblifestyle

Or send her an e-mail: nicky@discoveryourbounce.com

Failing to Succeed

Have you ever failed at something and felt your stomach sink? Have you ever had someone say to you, "How's business?" and answered with words and a smile that were fake?

I know I have.

You see I have walked the path of the entrepreneur, but in the beginning I had no idea that this was the route I had chosen.

I am a bright, educated, intelligent woman. I started my career in finance and spent 10 years learning about money. I am a Management Accountant after re-training once my girls came along, so I really know about money!

I have a strong and supportive family who encourage me to reach for my dreams, so when I decided to start my own business, although they were concerned that I was walking away from a good salary (which admittedly came at the price of my confidence and peace of mind), they wished me all the luck in the world.

My nickname in the early days was 'The Puppy'. Once I had an idea that was it, I was off in full-speed-ahead mode getting everything started. I had passion in heaps and wanted the whole wide world to know the benefits of using holistic therapies and following your intuition. I was evangelical, energetic and completely chaotic looking back.

I started by renting a room for my therapies and attending Mind, Body and Spirit events. Later I organised these events myself. Each one would have a catchy name, amazing graphics and I would work tirelessly; but at the end of every one I would put on my accountant head and compile a spreadsheet. This was the heart sinking moment – all that work and no money.

There were other failings too. My therapies and events were evenings and weekends whereas my husband worked 6am – 3pm. This was husband number two and I loved him so much all I wanted to do was be with him. Instead we were like ships passing in the kitchen – one in, one out. Was my business ever going to succeed if I was wishing I was at home?

As if the Universe heard my wishes I had the opportunity of setting up a therapy centre in a 3 way partnership. Again The Puppy was off, enthusiastically setting all systems to go with arrangements, Ikea purchases, wild ideas of events and happiness at having a base.

Again it worked…to a point. At 3 months in when 12 hour, 7 day weeks took their toll our relationship as partners fell apart. With no partnership agreement (who needs one of those, we're new best friends, right?) everything got messy and the ending of this business nearly took my sanity too.

I sat at home and licked my wounds. I listened to the mental chatter telling me of my shortcomings, flaws and wrong doings. I may as well have spent every day of that 3 months having coffee and buying shoes…I would have had more to show for it!

After some wallowing, I picked myself up, dusted myself off and got on with it. As I say I come from a supportive family so there were hugs, cups of tea and kindly words that shook off any feelings of pity for my situation. I set about finding somewhere to work from that was close to home and affordable where I could work school hours now that my children were approaching their final exams.

Once again the Universe delivered.

While buying a tent for my daughter's birthday the perfect space appeared. Two tiny joined conservatories on a small business estate with a café nearby. I had always had a dream of a holistic coffee shop and this was near enough for me. I had a therapy and reading room and a small shop selling crystal jewellery and I was in heaven.

After 7 months I felt ready for a new adventure and found another perfect space – my very own coffee shop! I had been dreaming of this since I started in business. For years I had uttered the words, "When I have my holistic coffee shop…" I knew the coffee we would serve, the cakes we would choose and how the space would be…every detail was alive in my mind's eye.

On the 10th April 2010 we opened our doors and again The Puppy surfaced! The stakes were high this time – this was my dream business after all. The decisions I had made about working to suit my lifestyle were forgotten and soon the evening and weekend working returned, but this time with full days too. The passion that I had in buckets sustained me for a while, but then the cracks started to appear.

My husband Phil is a saint and knew I loved my business, but I knew I was neglecting him and this made me sad. On days when my children were ill I was stuck manning the shop when my heart wanted to be with them giving them cuddles (even grown-ups need their Mummy when they are ill!).

My health suffered so badly that on a routine dive 3 months later I had a diving accident that caused a stroke. What followed was a long recovery period - a story to be told in another book I feel! We kept the shop going, but it was time and energy intensive and although this was my dream, the reality still lacked the magical elements I needed to be happy.

Once again I admitted failure and sold my shop. The money had been ok, but the overheads were high and the personal life price even higher. Somehow though this one didn't seem as hard to deal with. The voice on my shoulder didn't berate me or drag my feelings through the dirt, as there was inspiration coming to light about everything I had done so far.

Of course my stroke recovery had taught me much and the soul searching that went on had helped my inner calm. In addition my years as a business owner were now paying rewards.

Today, Discover Your Bounce is a group of companies that work to help people create a strong vision and the energy for life. Our team has grown and we have helped thousands of people by asking, "What does good look like?"

You see I now know the life of the entrepreneur, some have their own business and some flourish in a company environment. They call it a Hero's Journey for very good reason. You are driven by a passion and no other way will do. You know you can make a difference to the world and could not return to a 9-5 job, ever. Period.

Here's the most important thing. Every time I thought I was failing, I was actually succeeding. I was finding out who I am. I learned my strengths. I know my values. I gained new skills. I followed those who have gone before me and added my own talents.

I know what I don't want too – and sometimes that is an excellent place to start!

When you are travelling the country wishing you were at home your business will not work. When you are working out of your back bedroom yearning for the freedom of the open road that won't work either. If you are a night owl dragging yourself to morning networking you won't have the energy to create relationships and neither will morning people at evening events.

When you align your values, your skills and your hours with that great idea then you have found your recipe for success.

This great quote has really struck a chord with me:

"To succeed in life, you need three things: a wishbone, a backbone, and a funny bone." ~ Reba McEntire

Strength, aspiration and a sense of humour are the three things I wish I had consciously deployed when I started out on this journey. Laughing at our own frailties remind us that we are human and also engages the frontal lobe of the brain to solve problems. A backbone is needed when our fear grips us so that we keep on keeping on. As for a wishbone, well you can see how, when I knew what I wanted, the Universe repeatedly delivered.

When we are crystal clear on what we are setting out to achieve, the cogs and wheels stir to get us to our goals. When something doesn't work there is always a lesson in there too – what key element was missing that stopped the magic from happening?

Look back over your own life. Every time you 'failed' was there something beautiful that happened? Did you learn a new skill that proved invaluable on your next step?

Never be afraid to have a go, to take a step and give that thing a try, whatever it is. Trust that you will know if it's right and listen to your inner voice when really you know it's not for you. Try not to carry on regardless, be bold and brave and make your changes – your future self will thank you!

My mission is to help people who have a dream and keep it inside. I see people who are miserable where they are and think they have no choice. By having a go and even publicly failing, you give others inspiration by seeing that they don't have to be perfect. When they see you laugh at your early efforts and end up at a place of success they too may take that first step. They may even learn from you and not fail at all!.

Human Sustainability and the Art of Bounce!

We live in a world full of possibility. We have technology beyond anything we've known before. Modern science is advancing in leaps and bounds. At any moment we can access information, get translations for almost any language or simply find out where you've seen an actress before and why they look so familiar!

And yet…

The number of sick days taken increases by a couple of million per year. People take anti-depressants and are still depressed. People take sleeping tablets and lie awake all night.

Why is it that in an abundant world, we are so lacking in time, peace and vitality? How, in such a fast-changing world and uncertain economic time, are we going to not only find more of these three things, but also sustain them?

Who do you know that exudes peace and vitality? Are they selfish and grabbing? Or kind and generous? It seems to me that the healthiest and happiest of us do good deeds and give generously. So, my theory on how to save the future of our planet starts with you!

If you have previously read my story you will know that in 2010, I suffered a stroke after a scuba dive due to being time poor, stress rich and a series of very unhealthy life choices.

I know people look at me today and assume that my life is plain sailing now; that I'm always healthy, always happy and that no challenges occur for me. I wish that were true!

The truth is, since my dive accident I've had my fair share of tumbles, both physical and emotional.

From concussion and multiple injuries on a ski holiday, to a bout of pleurisy that got me admitted to hospital for a suspected heart attack. I've had financial challenges, business and family challenges. When the menopause entered my life, I spent eighteen months with headaches, weight gain, hot flushes and such a crisis of confidence I questioned everything from my business to my hair style.

It would have been easy during some of those dark times to ask, "Why me?" The fact is the more I've shared my stories, the more I've come to realise that most people have had one, or several, life defining challenges or traumas.

Instead of feeling hard done by, I've learned an important secret that allows me to embrace the future and whatever it brings...I've learned how to Bounce! In this chapter I'd like to share my secret with you too.

What does good look like to you? Some people call this resilience or wellbeing, some call it mojo or get up and go. My nicknames include 'Tigger' and 'The Bouncy Lady'. I quite often get calls from friends wanting support and advice in tough times and I love being able to help.

What I have learned is simple, but make no mistake, it isn't easy.

To learn how to bounce you first have to study yourself. You have to be able to spot your patterns. To look into yourself and your life and be really honest about when you make bad choices.

It could be that you are too hard on yourself. It could be that your self-talk really sucks. It could be that you suffered a trauma, or multiple traumas, in your childhood or younger years that made you afraid of someone or something in life. It could be that you have taken on a big challenge and given it your all, without boosting your energy first.

Or it could be something else entirely – every single one of us is unique, with unique experiences and a unique way of processing them.

The next step is to be open to change. You don't need to know how to change and you don't need all the answers. If you are feeling stuck or uncomfortable, it may feel impossible to imagine a better day. If you are open to life being different and open to trying a few things just in case they work, then that is a great place to start.

From here on the adventure begins! Once you have declared to the universe that you are ready for change, the next bit is magical – if you are watching. My favourite phrase from Goethe is:

"Whatever you do, or dream you can, begin it. Boldness has genius, power and magic in it."

The point is, you have to *do* something. You can read endless books, go on courses and attend seminars promising you everything from riches and wealth, to knowledge and health. But without action from *you* nothing changes.

There will be setbacks too, but if you passively accept them life won't get better. My advice? Intentional, repetitive action.

There are three main areas where, in my experience, focused change brings the most reward.

Boost Your Energy

We need energy to live. I see so many people 'just getting to Friday' and I hate that. This means they don't have the energy for their loved ones, or the fun stuff in their life. They get done the things on their 'to do' list, but this doesn't include making memories that they will look back on and smile. Will you remember that your desk was tidy, or your house was clean in ten years' time? Perhaps not!

To live a life full of excitement, happiness, or fulfilment (you choose), you need energy. This comes from good sleep, good nutrition, hydration and a positive environment. As I said, simple not easy! Life is fast and furious and if we don't plan in the elements for health first, the other stuff will take priority.

For example: I plan three weeks in advance for my fitness, two weeks in advance for friends, family and fun and a week in advance for healthy food. When I do this I feel amazing and when I don't the cracks start to appear!

Gratitude

Have you stopped to marvel at the amazing life we've been given? The beautiful planet full of trees, birds and animals? The changing seasons that each bring their own unique beauty to admire? A world that is constantly changing?

Have you thanked someone for their kindness? Or declared how good the day will be upon waking first thing? Or listed out all the good things that happened that day as you settle down to sleep?

When we are too busy or in a bad mood we grumble and complain. Spend any time at an airport or in a traffic jam and you will see this in action. When I'm tired I become really grumpy and win awards for my sarcasm!

However this isn't what I want to be known for and I'm very good at catching myself when this starts. By listing my gratitudes: thinking about my amazing children and grandchildren, my awesome husband or brilliant parents and brother I can snap myself out of a bad mood in a nanosecond. I can also just breathe in and spot something around me: a smiling child, a blue sky or a cute animal and I'm back to bouncing. It really is that simple…with practice!

Play

I've got so good at this! I re-discovered ballet after thirty-three years and I can still rock a turned-out leg. I've remembered that I love to swim. I found out that I am able to run (who knew?) and completed a 10k. I'm learning to indoor skydive in a wind tunnel.

Suffering that stroke could have been the end of my life with no notice – a fact my daughter made me stop and think about. I now make it a priority to spend as much time as I can with everyone that's important to me. Even if it's a quick message to say hello or a funny meme to make them smile, everything counts.

Remember what I said about consistency? Of course I get it wrong and you will too. What will also happen is that you will find, over time, you get it right more often than not. You will also find more people that support you as they see the changes for the better.

There will be some people that try to keep you stuck, or put you off for fear that they may need to change too. I have lost friends and colleagues over the years and of course that stings, but I have to do what's right for me and so do they.

The other great thing here is that the bouncier you feel the more time and energy you have, so you get to do more cool stuff. If you do face a challenge you will find that you bounce quicker, as you will remember to use the formula that works for you.

Remember I mentioned sustainability?

In my experience healthy, happy people (whom I call Bouncy people) make kind choices. They have a wealthy, abundant mindset and so are not driven to selfishly consume and covet. Living in gratitude means they want to pay it forward and create good times for everyone they meet; from opening a door for a struggling mum to buying a coffee for a homeless person.

Bouncy people will also step over an ant, take home their rubbish, recycle and reuse. I believe that with all that energy and a positive mindset, they may quite possibly save the planet in the process!

PAT MATTHEWS

Pat has been many things throughout her life, from civil servant to stay-at-home mum, to running the accounts and administration for the company she owns with her husband, Gerald, for over 35 years.

Her family has always been her priority – she's been a listening ear for all and has dispensed plenty of sage advice over the years. She's the matriarch of a very close knit and supportive family.

Her family asked her to take part in this book to share some of the experience that has helped them so much over the years, so others could benefit from it too.

You can reach Pat at:

Website: http://www.m-and-b-engineering.co.uk

E-mail: mandbeng@gmail.com

Counted Blessings

I have very happy memories of my childhood. My parents must have had really tough times bringing up three children in days of rationing, but as a child we didn't notice such things. It's only later you realise that your mum would go without food herself to give to you and your siblings and of course you believed her when she said she had eaten earlier.

All I remember are the good things. The walks with Mum & Dad after Sunday School, usually around the fields of Weston and Lansdown, up Blind Lane and across Cowslip Bank. Dad would pick watercress from a fresh bubbling spring to bring back for teatime sandwiches to go with the jelly and blancmange and we would pick flowers to take home too.

In those days there were carpets of primroses and cowslips and bluebells in Weston Woods at the far end of Broadmoor Lane. They seem to have disappeared in more recent years; maybe we picked them all!

I remember there was much more snow in the wintertime than we have these days. We would go tobogganing with my dad and often bring back wood from the farm for our coal fire. I have more good memories of evenings around the fire, I remember the toasting fork we used to make toast, sometimes dropping the bread into the fire and having to start again! Of course there was no television in those days…

I remember Christmas mornings, running into Mum and Dad's room for our presents only to be persuaded back to bed, as 'he hadn't been yet'. I later found out that they had got to bed at 2am after finishing the painting and stitching on my beautiful pushchair!

We were awake again at 7am and I still remember my gorgeous pushchair with floral pillows and covers, it had such a lovely smell!

The year of the doll's house Dad made was really special, I'm still not sure where it was hidden. It was 4 feet tall, painted white with a red roof, with 2 floors and furniture throughout. It was large enough for my brother and I to hide in and read stories with a torch!

At that time there were three of us, 2 girls and a boy. After 11 years my parents had a very much unplanned bonny baby boy weighing 10lbs!

I remember my mother saying she was embarrassed to be pregnant at her age and worried about what people might think. It seems funny now, but it was 1955, she was 35 years old and things were very different then.

My baby brother Nigel brought so much love into our lives and he was very special to us all. I was 13 and thought it the most wonderful present, hurrying home from school for cuddles and delighting in being with him. I was even allowed to 'lay in' on Saturday mornings to give him his bottle while Mum got the housework done. My sister and I fought to feed him, bath him and change his nappies – even the challenging ones!

Nigel was the centre of our family life and we all doted on him. I always feel he brought so much to our lives in those special years and the caravan holidays in Devon hold such wonderful memories.

When I went out to work, I would buy him a present on payday, sometimes clothes or toys, but I loved to spoil him. He was very clever at school and had numerous friends. I remember taking him to see The Jungle Book, just Nigel and me and we danced all the way from the bus to our house singing, "I wanna be like you hoo hoo!"

I got married in 1962 to Gerald and in February 1970 I had Nicola (the compiler of this book), my first baby. It was a long and difficult breach birth where we almost lost her.

Nigel thought the world of Nicola! I spent a lot of time at my Mum's house in the day and Nigel would play with her and give her a cuddle when he came home from school. I remember him walking around nursing and cuddling her the day of her first injection when she really wasn't happy!

On the 14th of September that same year, Nigel had a terrible accident and died in Frenchay hospital from a head injury.

We were all numb with shock. My parents were heartbroken; he was the last child at home and the centre of their lives. They slept the next 6 weeks at our home – nights in their own house were just too upsetting. Days were spent with things to sort and arrangements to be made but generally we were all in a haze. Mum & Dad busied themselves with anything they could, but Nicola gave them a focus and a purpose. They loved her to bits anyway but she really came into her own at that time. She was very 'knowing' and I always said she had been here before!

The day of Nigel's funeral at 7 months old she sat bolt upright in her pram with no cushions – she had never done that before. It's funny the things you remember.

One night shortly after when I was too upset to sleep I sat in the living room and wrote a poem to Nigel. It was a full A4 sheet and the words just came tumbling out. I felt at the time that someone was helping me write this poem. I only ever showed it to my husband, because it was too upsetting and heartfelt to show to my mum. Years later, when I would have shown it to her I couldn't find it, but we both still remember how poignant that poem was.

I still say losing Nigel was the most horrible, difficult thing that has ever happened in my life and find it inconceivable that 'God' or 'The Universe' could have ever needed him as much as we did.

I coped at the time, busy with family life and tried not to talk about Nigel because I couldn't without crying and the only person I would cry in front of was my husband. So I kept my emotions at bay not to upset Mum and Dad even more.

It was 5 years later, in the village with my son Darren in the pushchair, when a lady approached me about Nigel and the floodgates opened. I couldn't speak, I just sobbed and she was so sorry to have upset me. All I could do was mumble an apology through the tears and hurry away.

With hindsight, the lesson I think I learned was that counselling at the time of losing Nigel would have helped all of us. When it was suggested we declined, thinking we would find solace in our own family. We then feared upsetting each other and these emotions were buried so deeply. We think we have dealt with them but they are still there.

With counselling, talking freely to an unconnected person can release a lot of the hurt, anger and sadness and maybe it would have helped us to find peace. As it was, we did our best; we pulled together and took one step after the other. Our family was never the same but we all loved each other dearly and although my parents aren't here today I am proud of my upbringing.

Time is a great healer and the good memories do diminish the bad ones in time, I am glad that I got 14 wonderful years with Nigel rather than not knowing him at all. I constantly count my blessings. I have a wonderful, loving husband of 53 years, 2 lovely children, who make me extremely proud and four gorgeous grandchildren. They have all given me endless love and happiness.

We are all very close and constantly in touch with each other, a day doesn't pass without a visit, call or text. I am very lucky, not only do I get hugs from my husband and children; I also get cuddles from my grandchildren.

How blessed am I?

Life's Reflections

When I was asked to write a second chapter I wasn't sure what to write about. I then thought about the one thing that has supported me through my life: the relationship with my family and friends. We have just stepped into another new year, so it's the perfect time to look back on my life and what has happened over my years on the planet.

I find New Year in particular to be very emotional. Over the last few years, as 12 o'clock comes, my close friend Eileen and I can barely speak for tears. They aren't sad tears really: it's just a time when we reflect on people we have lost, but more so that we appreciate the family we have and feel totally blessed.

We just hug each other with emotion, not needing words. Then my husband Gerald and I have the biggest hug ever!

New Year is a time of reflection and gratitude. It's when I think of times past and childhood days growing up in a loving family. We had selfless parents who did everything to make our lives happy.

I think too, of the really happy times bringing up my own children. Truly the best of times!

Then later, sharing the grandchildren who brought with them another dimension to love. Gerald and I have watched on as they have all grown into adults and still love to hear their news. In particular I cherished the times after school, sharing stories on the way home and den making in our living room. It's amazed me the extra patience I have with grandchildren!

We are so lucky to still have each other and love one another more and more as time goes on. We also cherish our close family. Any problems, however traumatic (as sometimes they are) draw us closer. We as a family always deal with things together, whichever one is struggling at the time. There have been very difficult situations, but these only cement our family even closer.

Gerald and I are still working, running the engineering company that we started in 1981. Gerald manages the day to day, employing four people and running the office, while I deal with the accounts, VAT and admin.

We also enjoy our leisure time. We love our time together; whether that's at home, occasionally going out with friends or spending good times at our caravan by the sea.

The static caravan was our best venture, giving us a place to 'jump off' any weekend to totally chill. We walk by the sea, visit lots of different interesting places in Dorset and Devon and spend happy times, with a whole new set of like minded friends. Oh and share a glass or two!

To top all that, we have great holidays with our family in Europe, America and the Caribbean. These are really special and I can't wait to discover what's next on the agenda for the coming summer of 2020!

In September 2019 life got even better as we had a very welcome addition to our family, a new great grandchild who brings even more love into our lives!

What was I saying about being blessed? We are truly surrounded by blessings!

SHARON CRITCHLOW

Sharon is one to watch! As an international best-selling writer and speaker Sharon is a vocal changemaker. She brings passion to the subjects of the future of work, diversity, emotional intelligence and environmental social governance.

Sharon is a qualified Accountant with over 20 years of experience in senior leadership roles and growing successful businesses. Within Discover Your Bounce, Sharon looks after the finances and provides strategic direction for the group. She is a popular conference speaker as well as regularly creating and facilitating workshops. A qualified coach and mentor, Sharon is passionate about people becoming the best that they can be and allowing their true talents to shine.

In her spare time Sharon is an Advocate for the Association of Chartered Certified Accountants (ACCA) encouraging people in to the profession and supporting their development. She also enjoys music and has been known to play the flute and sing – although not at the same time!

Website: www.discoveryourbounce.com

Email : Sharon@discoveryourbounce.com

Linkedin: www.linkedin.com/in/sharoncritchlow

Twitter: @sharoncritchlow

Choosing My Outcome

The thought of writing this made me laugh, then cry, then laugh again. I am surrounded by amazing people who have overcome all manner of physical and emotional traumas to truly shine. Cancer, stroke, and abuse have been present in the lives of my dearest friends and I'm blessed that none of those outcomes have been in my life to date. What did I have to bounce back from?

Growing up in a small seaside town in the South West of England I had great summers, countless days on the beach and all the fun experiences that happen when you are a teenager working in cafes and hotels. I also had an ineffective education. In the beginning I didn't realise this, or understand what was wrong. The bullying didn't help, the lack of teaching staff didn't help, but I always felt something else was missing. In the early years I was very shy, I didn't like to say I didn't understand and whilst my confidence grew in many areas, I still couldn't bring myself to admit it, but at 16 I struggled to read.

In the 1980's exams weren't necessary to get a job. My hard working parents were pleased with the few exams I passed and I was congratulated upon my success. At the same time I was all too aware that at times, Mum had three jobs and Dad worked twelve hours a day. For them, life was a daily struggle to provide for us. Watching people enjoying the lovely yachts in the town marina, having the freedom to travel and experience the world on their own terms seemed an unrealistic dream for me. Totally unobtainable.

At 17 I had a breakthrough; I had an eye test and became the owner of some lovely large bright green glasses. I wore them for the first time when I left the opticians and took the train home. I will always remember the tears in my eyes; for the first time in my life I could read the billboards on the platform. I confess to feeling cheated, but I resolved to tackle the reading issue. It was a slow process at first but daily reading practice ensued and reading is now one of my true pleasures in life. At 18 I left full time education having struggled through college, leaving with low grades in my A levels. I had started to believe that my lack of success was because I had reached my intellectual limit, but deep down that didn't feel right.

I had energy and enthusiasm, but was facing an impossible task. I didn't want a life of financial hardship, so I needed a career with prospects. With reading not being my strong point I went for numbers. I decided to be an accountant. I quickly learned that not everyone will share your vision. Their comments are often a reflection of the restrictions they place on their own lives and their fears for you. I heard that "People like us don't become accountants" and "Don't be too disappointed when you fail." One of the great things about having nothing to lose is that you may as well have a go at the unobtainable. As few things are truly unobtainable and, in having a go you never know what you may discover.

In the first few years in work I made many discoveries.

In the beginning I discovered that over a hundred letters to local accountants and solicitors yielded two interviews, at one of which they appeared most disappointed at my female form - they were clearly expecting a chap! In fact, I only got replies to letters signed 'S Critchlow', no replies to those letters signed 'Miss S Critchlow.' I also learned that having the name of my school on my CV was more of a hindrance than a help. However, persistence paid off.

I took a position as a filing clerk in an accountancy practice and filed documents really quickly, so that they would have to teach me something new for the rest of the day. After a summer of filing and some help from my mum, I moved to a small firm of accountants that needed someone who was happy to start at the bottom. University wasn't an option for me, so I studied for professional qualifications as I worked and hit an intellectual brick wall. The books were huge! My ability to learn from them was small!

The one day per week at college reminded me of the frustrations of school and I had a similar result. The exams were three hours each at degree level - one year in and I had passed one exam with fourteen left to go. This clearly wasn't working. I asked my employer if he would fund some weekend courses instead. The budget was tight so I chose a small, less expensive college – 200 miles away. This meant I spent one weekend a month away from home, studying.

In the end it took nearly four years but I'm so glad that I went. I met a trainer who showed me how to learn without re writing the book and how to give the examiners what they wanted. This was a revelation. I practiced past papers and the mind mapping technique of using diagrams to organise information presented on the courses and before long – armed with large sheets of paper and colouring pens - I mastered it. It took me eighteen months to pass the next four exams and two and a half years to pass the next ten. I passed the final three after only three months of study.

At 23 I qualified as an Accountant with the Association of Chartered Certified Accountants. (ACCA). For me, it was a major achievement and turning point in my life. From this point I was able to move forward with more confidence, knowledge and pace.

At 23 I could not have predicted that over the next twenty years I would go on to pass more exams, become a member of a number of prestigious organisations and alongside my partners build a multi-million pound business. However, I knew things would be different and be better. What I learned about myself in those years would see me through many tough times ahead. I learned much more than accountancy.

I learned that:

- There is no such thing as setting the bar too high - just keep yourself on track with bite sized achievable goals. Congratulate yourself on each goal achieved and when you lose the will to carry on – re-cap what you have achieved to date and remind yourself how far you have come.
- Years of not seeing the blackboard at school gave me a wonderful talent to remember the spoken word. This is really useful in meetings and goes to demonstrate that early setbacks can give rise to unique skills!
- I could have been written off at age 18 as having reached the pinnacle of my academic abilities. Whilst the professional exams were much harder than A levels, I learned that exams at 16 and 18 tend to be content based, requiring extensive recall of facts with basic analysis. Whereas the more senior professional exams award more marks for understanding how each of these areas come

together and interact. For me my true talents are in problem solving. When I see people who struggle with lower level exams I tell them to stick with it, as they could have a brain that solves problems easily and as the exams progress they can increasingly play to their strengths.

- I have discovered that learning is not a linear thing; you can have a breakthrough at any stage, you may just need a different approach.
- The more I tried, the more people stepped forward to help with the tools I needed. I learned that those who succeed weren't always those with natural talent - more often they were those who wanted it the most and were prepared to keep going – even with a 400 mile round trip.
- Things not going well? Chat over how you feel with someone who has been there before, someone who shares your passion for the project, or someone who shares all of your passions. Let others pace for you to get you across the line. It will still be your success. I have learned to ask for help and that if you are committed to the outcome, others will help.
- Be patient with those who do not see your vision. Whether it is prejudice against your background or your gender, or well-meaning words which are aimed at protecting you, but deflate your dreams - remember that sometimes the world is just like that. It says everything about them and nothing about you – unless you decide to own it. Whatever you are telling yourself will dictate your future, not whatever they are saying to you - so have faith in your abilities. Only you will truly know how much you want this.

Finally, remember this: the world is full of infinite possibilities and outcomes. With all of those possibilities available to you, you may as well choose your own outcome.

Good luck!

Hiding the Humanist

The previous chapter was my first foray into writing and as with any new venture there comes excitement, trepidation and a period of reflection. It was first released as part of a book which became an international best seller and I watched it on its release date scale the Amazon charts from my iPad on my desk at work.

At work I was stressed and under constant pressure, not just from the demands of the role but also a less than ideal working arrangement with my business partners. The book gave me the opportunity to consider where I had come from, but also where I was at that time and where I really wanted to be.

For many years I felt I was two very different people, co-habiting one body. One side of me is a business person, an accountant. I like puzzles, numbers and structure. The other side of me is a free thinker, a humanist and a caring, sharing Buddhist. When I was at work I spent a lot of energy hiding the humanist, only to find she emerged whenever there was a crisis! She mended up relationships and encouraged people, but always on the quiet. When I was in my early 30's something happened which gave the humanist in me a new insight, one which I will be forever grateful for.

My first 32 years

Until I was 32 I had the "perfect figure". I was a size 12 and I hardly thought about my body at all. I had been a Latin American dancer alongside my accountancy career and enjoyed everything dance related. Then one day I got a stomach virus... It changed my life. I spent a week struggling to eat and felt drained and lethargic.

Whilst my appetite returned, the feeling of exhaustion stayed with me for 10 years. I had developed Post-Viral Fatigue (PVF). My body ached constantly and the slightest physical activity made me exhausted. To this day I need to be aware of what my body needs and balance my energy to avoid a relapse.

The impact

At a time when PVF and M.E. were not widely recognised, I was left to sort out my situation with no medical support. I realised that if I ate more sugar I got a bit more energy, which kept my brain going long enough for me to keep working. The impact was that my size 12 body became a size 16 body. I didn't know how to dress it, I didn't like what it looked like and I often hid. People weren't very kind. From comments about the size of my behind, to remarks such as, "It must be really hard when you had this fabulous body."

I struggled for years living half a life. Having holidays where all I did was sleep, focusing only on the business, ignoring my body and living in my head. My world got smaller.

By August 2015 I had enjoyed a successful 20-year commercial career, a six-figure income, a half functioning body and a broken spirit. As I was watching the book rise in the charts I decided I needed a change; I wanted to bring my whole self to everything I did. I had watched so many people be gobbled up and spat out by the commercial world, living on backbiting and half-truths. I could see that no-one was winning. But who was going to say it? I was looking at a generation of executives fuelled by pills and booze and the next generation was loath to commit to joining us. Who could blame them?

Bounce

Having sold the shares in that business, I was asked by Nicky Marshall to be her Non- Executive Director in Discover Your Bounce. This gave me both a focus and a challenge. At that time Discover Your Bounce was a personal development business. I loved the programme and I started to wonder if there was something we could do to have a wider impact on the burnout we both saw in business. To bring in wider wellbeing which I knew that Nicky and I both had personal experience with. This was ideal for me as both sides of me got to play. The problem for me was that I had to reveal the humanist: she had learned a powerful skill from the illness and that skill was going to be vital in making this work.

Fears emerged around my credibility and whether I would be valued or accepted if I let the humanist in me shine. Through the experience of PVF I now understand what it is to be human in a way I could never have imagined before. The skill was empathy. In this changing and increasingly digitalised world, I believe our inner human is what we each bring to the party. Our creativity, our ethics, our empathy and ability to inspire and work together to produce greater things are all human traits. We all have them. As computing takes over the mundane, these parts of ourselves become more valuable and commercially and we need to access them in our teams and in ourselves. The empathy grew into studying and understanding Emotional Intelligence as a whole. Bringing my commercial and physical experiences together to find a more sustainable path in business. My role emerged as a speaker, coach, mentor and facilitator.

"How can you stand there when you look so fat?"

As with all changes, there are times when you are tested. A poignant one for me came in 2018. I was hosting a pop-up for our wellbeing business in a branch of HSBC. A lady approached the stand and asked to speak to me in private. She asked me, "How can you stand there when you look so fat?" Emotional Intelligence tells us it is our choice how we respond.

27 year old Sharon would have slapped her, 37 year old Sharon would have been in tears, but 47 year old Sharon asked her a question:

"What is it about fat that you don't like?"

Her response? "I'm not as fat as you, but I can barely leave the house because of it and yet you just stand there with no shame."

I will come onto shame later. We all too often receive personal comments which are actually just a reflection of someone else's state of mind. I'm sure we have all compared ourselves to others at some time and decided we are not worthy, or lacking in some way. The challenge is to dig deeper and recognise and embrace your true self. It's easy to accept other peoples' negative narrative, but do you embrace the positive comments you receive in the same way? Do you truly understand and embrace what your uniqueness brings to humanity? This is empathy in action. This potentially negative situation has now become one of my stories I tell when I'm speaking about Emotional Intelligence. I will be forever grateful to her.

What I have learned about me

My change in body shape has allowed me to be more body aware; it has given me insights into societal attitudes that I was unaware of before. I have grown to respect my body. I still ache at times, but every day holds joy for me. The lady in HSBC was right: I'm not ashamed of my body. Through this experience I now understand what it is to be human. As lessons go, it was a hard one, but one I would not change as what I have learned holds more value to me. This humanist now has a mission, the skills to support it and a wonderfully curvaceous size 16 body with which to deliver it.

At 32 I was afraid of public speaking, I hid from confrontation and I was fearful of not being accepted. Now I more readily recognise fear and shame in others and have found ways of providing support I had not considered important before. All of my relationships have a deeper quality, especially the one with myself. By accepting and embracing the whole of me I am no longer so self-conscious.

I truly understand why we all have an equal place in society. I now speak on a range of business and Emotional Intelligence related topics and my only concern is that my audience gets some value from what I am saying. This humanist now has a voice! I now bring both sides of me together to fulfil a bigger purpose.

There is no shame in being me. There is no shame in being you either.

Your value cannot be weighed on scales, only felt in the hearts of others.

PART TWO

ADRIAN CHASE

Adrian is an author, speaker, podcast presenter and personal coach. Adrian works with his clients to help them fulfil their potential, enabling whatever that means to them.

In Adrian's words:

"Most of us live our lives in a very different way to how we did thousands of years ago but one thing hasn't changed: the primary function of the brain is to alert us to threats to our survival. It's made me realise how powerful and important social connection is.

The most basic of all human needs is the need to understand and be understood."

Throughout my life I have had various careers. Only one thing has never changed and that is the idea of helping people with the way they 'think'. Emotional connection if you like. It's called **sharing**.

Surely Lightning Never Strikes Twice?

Some 20 years ago now, a pretty typical early morning had just begun. I was an Area Manager at the time, working for a national chain of newsagent shops and my area covered the home counties outside of Central London. I'd been there so long there probably wasn't an issue I hadn't already experienced.

It was a typical British November morning. As I left home at 4am to arrive at the shop for 5am the sky was still dark; the air cold and damp. The shop had some 40 paper rounds, which took a lot of organising and staff. Two of the staff were adults who used vehicles for the outlying drops and the newspaper boys and girls took out the rest which were local to the branch.

As we were delivering in Gerrards Cross, virtually all the papers were broadsheets and 20 of those were more than enough for anyone to carry!

The marking up shed, as it was called, was actually a brick building probably the size of a double garage. It sat adjacent to the back door of the shop and was kitted out with tables to accommodate the large quantity of newspapers. Once the rounds had all gone it was then my job to transfer the papers from the 'shed' to the front display in the shop ready for customers to purchase. This is the way it would happen seven days a week over many years of trading.

Using a shopping trolley to move the papers into the shop, I would unlock the backdoor and push the shopping trolley into the stockroom. I would then lock the door behind me and push the papers to the front of the shop. It was a simple enough task but would take about six trips normally to clear the papers from one point to the other. I was about to realise that this simple task would lead to, for me, a life changing event.

The time was now about 5.45am. The sky still dark, the air still cold and damp outside. At this point there was no one about, other than probably every other newsagent up and down the country.

With my third load onboard, I unlocked the back door of the shop and started to push the trolley in. No sooner than I had done that I heard people running towards me screaming and shouting, swearing at me to get on the floor.

I was completely disorientated by this and still trying to take in what was happening. By this time they were right next to me; screaming at me to get on the floor with my face down. The shop was being robbed.

As I lay on my front I began to shake. Not uncontrollably, but it would have been too strong to suppress. I was thinking how this must be what people mean when they describe the shock as setting in. I was still not aware of how many people were in the shop. I knew there was the one holding me down with a shotgun pointed at me, ensuring I wouldn't move.

He said to me, "It will only be a few minutes and then we will be gone so best you just keep quiet and everything will be ok."

Could you imagine how you would react if this ever happened to you? I'd seen it in films and thought about it once or twice before. Never did I imagine I would experience it for real. At the time I was in self-protection mode and remained compliant, as it would have been futile to try anything else.

I remained completely silent, looking at his trainers and noticed they were bright blue with white laces. That's worth remembering I thought.

I could hear the rest of the gang in the shop and could only assume that they were *attacking* the cigarette gantry to get the security shutter open. At retail value the stock was worth about £5,000 so probably worth half of that on the black market. I can remember lying there thinking the best I could do was to remember everything I could and recall as much as possible to the police after this was over.

After what seemed a lifetime, although probably only four or five minutes in reality, the other gang members came into the stockroom. They told my *guard* to get me into the office and sit me on a chair, which he did. I can remember starting to feel anger towards them, for what they were putting me through. All wearing ski masks and pretty non-descript clothing, so I concentrated on the footwear and ski masks.

I proceeded to open the safe as requested and they took the small amount of cash left inside. Luckily, we use a bank night safe, so there wasn't much in there for them to take. I was surprised they didn't query the amount in a way. They took the rest of the cigarettes and told me to stay in the office and not contact anyone because they would know. They ran out of the branch back door and I heard them start up the car. They drove off down the back road running behind the shops.

I didn't wait. I contacted the police immediately who said they would attend as soon as possible.

I was standing in the office thinking over what had just happened. I was trying to deal with the trauma and sort out how I was going to operate the shop. I didn't expect customers to understand. The police had said not to open the shop until Scenes of Crime Operatives had been.

I tried to carry on as per normal and went back out into the 'shed' to start moving the newspapers again. One of the adult delivery drivers was back and of course had seen or heard nothing of the robbery but could tell I wasn't myself. I told him of the robbery and what had just happened and I can remember putting my head in my hands and thinking, "These things don't happen to me." I felt like I was living out one of my worst nightmares.

I went back into the office and he made me a cup of tea. While there, I looked for my car keys so I could move my car. The keys were not where I had left them on top of the office filing cabinet. I briefly looked around and then realised that someone in the gang had taken them with him. I felt totally abused and stuck with having to field yet another trauma.

I phoned my boss to explain what had happened.

His main question was, "When do you think the shop will be open?"

That taught me all I needed to know about the way he thought. From that moment, I guess I always knew that we would part company at some point in the future. I needed those around me who, in a situation like this, could offer physical support.

The police came and I described the event. They asked me if my boss had offered me counselling.

I replied by saying "It's ok, I will be fine."

Feeling that this would be a one off event I spent the next days trying to get everything into perspective. Looking back now it was difficult for me to do that on my own. I didn't realise the value of counselling back then.

Approximately three weeks later I decided to go and open the branch again on a Saturday morning. The routine was the same as before, only we now had security cameras so you could see anyone there outside the back door.

Of course having the security cameras makes no difference to the people that know the lie of the land. They especially don't care if masked. They may have also recognised I was the person there before.

I couldn't believe it. That morning was a complete replay of the previous robbery. The running at me, the shouting and swearing, making me lie down on the floor. No reassuring words from my *guard* this time as I knew the drill. I turned to look at the shoes, which were the same blue trainers with white laces!

This just added to the trauma and this time I became almost belligerent which was a dangerous state of mind. When they left, I felt an anger that I had never felt before. Anger so strong that had it been directed towards my attackers I would not have cared for my physical outcome or theirs. This was to be a moment of learning for me. I had to forgive but I didn't need to forget.

Looking back now, I realise that for me, someone else having the power to choose over your life or death can actually make the post trauma very difficult to deal with. Not many will experience this. It has left me frightened of what my reaction would now be in a similar situation. I have never had dreams or nightmares but I can't help but wonder if my handling of emotions changed over that period.

Now that I have had the chance to put some distance in time between this trauma and how I am right now, there are some strengths that I now know I have since this event.

I realise that what they put me through wasn't personal. They didn't know me. They had never, before the first time, even met me before. They actually didn't care in any case, they just didn't think about the lasting consequences of how the robbery might affect me. I have learned to protect myself, my feelings, by making sure I never take comments or opinions from other people personally.

I now know that I can forgive and that doesn't mean I need to forget. I have learned never to bring back the feelings connected to bad memories but learn from these experiences.

I now know that all I need to do is bring back the feelings of good memories. Memories where I was at my best, my strongest and live in that moment.

Now that's powerful.

ALEXANDRA STUMPP

A 2019 graduate of German from the University of Bristol, Alex is the Events and Marketing Assistant for Discover Your Bounce. She joined the team in March 2019 as an Intern and is now a full-time employee. Her expertise is the study of cultures and languages. Being half Swiss and through her studies she speaks fluent German.

Learning new ways she can help her friends and family, as well as make a difference in the world will always be an ambition in her life. The second, is to own a dog and experience all that this amazing planet has to offer.

Email: Alex@discoveryourbounce.com

LinkedIn: Alexandra Stumpp

Welcome to Germany: F**k You All

The room was buzzing with all of us students chatting about our Year Abroad plans. The Year Abroad coordinator was about to give us the low-down on what would happen.

His first sentence was, "This is not a gap year. You have to work hard." He proceeded to talk about our responsibilities and procedures to follow when working and living abroad. Telling us that it would be a difficult year, but there were support systems in place.

The room fell silent. It was almost like we were a game of whack-a-mole and he decided to bring down the reality hammer. All those jumping with excitement were suddenly still. I knew this was not the intention; it was merely to remind us not to waste the year. To work hard and gain some valuable life experience. Either way, a lot of us left that lecture deflated and the nerves kicked in hard.

I, on the other hand, when walking into the Year Abroad meeting that day, was excited. My original plan was to work with a distant relative in her family business. I was going to be living close to Munich, getting re-acquainted and learning about my family roots in Bavaria. I felt like nothing could go wrong because I would have this amazing support system of family around me. I thought the lows they were referring to wouldn't happen to me. I was going to Germany, this would be easy because I'm half Swiss and having grown up in Basel for the first 8 years of my life, I'm used to living in a German speaking country.

September 5th 2017. I arrived into Germany.

My mother had kindly decided to drive me from the UK to Germany and within 10 minutes of driving onto the German Autobahn we saw a graffitied road sign that says, "F**k you all".

"Well that's a bad sign." We laughed it off, my excitement had not yet faded.

It wasn't until I arrived at my accommodation, which was arranged for me through work, that the excitement turned to fear. I was greeted by a lovely 40 year old Romanian man and living with him wasn't what scared me at the time: it was the fact that he only spoke Romanian and Italian. So communication was going to be hard to non-existent. Then I heard that there was no WIFI, no washing machine in the flat and after I asked no kettle. Now it's hard to believe how much comfort a kettle can make in a situation such as this; how the sound of the kettle boiling in the background actually reminds you of home.

Growing-up part British, if anything goes wrong, we put the kettle on.

I went from my home comforts and familiar faces, to limited communication and no Netflix to distract me from the fact that I was scared and alone. I thought I had chosen the best option, as I didn't have to go through the hassle of finding private accommodation.

Turns out I made the wrong choice.

Initially the living conditions were manageable. The town I was living in was quiet, idyllic and the big lake at the centre offered that connection to nature we all crave as human beings. I loved spending time at the lake, it just had to be time spent alone.

As the months passed, something was missing.

Ever since the day my mother left to go back to the UK, leaving me to embark on my adventure abroad, my excitement dwindled down from 100-0. I couldn't understand why. My job to begin with was new and challenging. I was surrounded by distant relatives and I made a friend in a co-worker.

Still, there was something missing.

I felt like I was existing and not living. I was struggling to make deep connections and found all my new connections were actually surface level. I didn't feel part of that community.

I thought I couldn't change my situation, reminding myself of the Year Abroad coordinator's talk. I had a duty to fulfill while abroad and I couldn't just run away. Especially since I had already finished two years of University and I didn't want to throw away my hard work.

I felt very stuck and extremely alone, to the point where I had a week or so of just uncontrollable tears, followed by a month of utter sadness and lack of motivation to even get out of bed. I would pull myself together for work, but then once back home and alone, I would sink back down into an empty hole again.

I tried walking around the lake and being in nature, but again I was alone. Watching the happy families and couples reminded me of what I was missing in my life. In my free time I was counting down the days until I could go back home again or until I had a visit from my boyfriend. My family and friends were only aware of some of it, as I hated telling them about something that they couldn't help me with. Meaning I wasn't following all the advice given to us in those talks.

That isn't to say that, on some days, I did take his advice about keeping friends and family close, but once I eventually open up to them, they became worried. They wanted me to talk to my German family, but the family were still strangers to me. I felt like I would be a burden on their already busy lives. After talking to family and friends back in the UK, I knew I was the only one that could get myself out of this hole I had fallen into.

I realised that the situation I currently found myself in was all my own doing. I chose to study German because it involved a year abroad. I chose the easy way and used my family connections to get me set up with an internship and a flat. I never put myself forward or created my own opportunities.

So I re-assessed.

I reflected on when am I happiest; when do I feel I have purpose?

I love to learn about culture I thought. I love being active in nature, being creative and meeting new people.

I knew I couldn't do this anymore at my current job. I had no real purpose there. As beautiful as the village was, I had no joy from work and no real friends.

First, I had to find a new place to live.

I found a place to live closer to Munich, with housemates who spoke German. I thought, this is it, it will get better. Especially since a work colleague introduced me to her daughter who was a similar age, meaning I had gained another friend.

The problem with the new house was that I still couldn't connect with the housemates and the strict landlord would come over unannounced and shout at me for pointless things. It left me feeling unsafe and uncomfortable in my own house. I had WIFI at least, but that didn't help as it only allowed me to escape my misery, rather than get out of a place I now realise I felt permanently anxious in.

Time to learn a new skill because I knew that makes me happy.

I started going to the library and reading some books about social media marketing. Visiting museums in Munich, going to Café's just to get out of the house. I was getting out of the house, but not out of my misery. Even though I had a new friend, she was understandably busy leading her own life, so I only saw her once a week.

Although this helped, I still wasn't out of the dark hole I felt I was in. During the week I would still go to work every morning to a place which wasn't the right fit for me.

My next decision was to change more than one thing in my life. I started looking for new internships as well as another place to live.

I decided to take a risk. A work colleague said they would take me on in their office for two months filing documents until I found a more permanent internship. Knowing my duty towards the University was fulfilled for the time being, I quit the internship early.

Those two months filing felt like they went on forever.

I was starting to lose hope that my time filing documents would end and I still wouldn't have found an internship. This could ruin my degree. Panic set in. I was applying nearly every day and the rejection letters were coming in quick.

Eventually, with only a few weeks left filing, I found an internship as a translation manager. After relentless searching and not giving up, my risk paid off.

This time I was going to go through the hassle of finding private accommodation in a new city called Kassel.

I had never heard of the city, but oh did it deliver! In Kassel I had to move twice within the space of 4 months. Regardless, my time there was as colourful and bright as the rows of ornately decorated houses that filled the city.

Working as a translation manager was challenging, but the right challenge. Rather than stress and dread, it was excitement and support from a team who were equipped with the time and resources to take an intern on. My time there was brilliant from start to finish and I left with first class references and even something I could go back and do for future work.

In terms of the people I met, there were still no deep connections, but I had housemates. This time I felt confident. So, if no- one was around, I could happily go and explore on my own.

Upon reflection, I did learn some truly valuable life lessons.

The first 6 months were not amazing, there was a time where I hit rock bottom and nearly threw away two years of hard work.

This isn't to say *every day* in those 6 months was difficult or lonely. In between I had made some great memories and had some exciting and funny times too. I just couldn't see it at the time because there weren't enough of them and the time in between felt too dark. There was still too much loneliness, not enough job satisfaction and I didn't feel like I was properly engaging with life.

Now I know that if something is missing in life, but one or two aspects of life are fine, that isn't reason to settle. Find what drives your happiness and complete it.

I remembered I did still have a choice and as my mother always told me, *"Where there is a will, there is a way."* After making changes and engaging with the world again I found my way out. It was my determination and willingness to take calculated risks, as well as doing the uncomfortable, that turned my year around.

The good times in Munich and Kassel, along with the amazing people, will never be forgotten. In fact, the way I developed my professional and personal character throughout the difficult times was an invaluable learning experience in itself and I am glad it happened to me.

Life isn't easy, the ride not always smooth. After experiencing a low so deep I hadn't felt before and managing to turn it around completely; I feel more equipped to say, "World, bring it on."

ALYSON HURST

Alyson is the parent of two grown up girls. She has lived in Bristol for twenty years. She travels to Swansea regularly to spend time with her father and at her favourite place, the sea.

She became a beekeeper in 2013 and is now the successful owner of Hives and Herbals. She sells beeswax products from her home and through several shops in Bristol.

Another important place in her life is Bristol Buddhist Centre. She attends classes there on a regular basis and manages to go away on study and meditation retreats several times a year.

Website: https://www.hivesandherbals.com

Facebook: https://www.facebook.com/hivesandherbals/

Instagram: https://www.instagram.com/hivesandherbals/

You Tube: https://www.youtube.com/channel/UC0BtKQYTT-3wikawio1Z0rA?view_as=subscriber

The Buddha and the Bees – Life's What You Make It

As a child growing up in a Welsh village on the edge of Swansea, life was pretty ordinary. We didn't have much money but had a lot of love and family was important. Everything seemed quite straightforward.

Some of my best memories were made at the beach, where we used to holiday in Gower. It was there my love and connection with the sea began, one which I still carry with me today. I can still close my eyes and picture the free little girl with her wet salt-water ponytails. I felt at ease, I felt complete freedom and contentment.

Who knew what life had in store for me at that time? Needless to say, the beach is where I want to go to find calm and freedom, or to release rage. For me, the sea expresses it all.

Without really thinking about it I had that vision of what family life would be in my head. I wanted to recreate those memories for my own family, so after being married for a short while we started trying for a baby.

From here the path started to diverge and the challenges began.

Things didn't go to plan and we ended up at an infertility clinic. Even the name of it was painful – infertility rather than fertility. A small point to many, but very important to me. As a couple we became a walking womb and sperm producer. We went through what felt like very clinical processes with little emotional support being offered.

Everyone around us started giving us advice, but the most helpful conversation I had at this time was with my sister. She said she had no idea what I was going through, but she was always there for me to talk to. I held on to her message of understanding and it brought me great comfort.

I remember the deep disappointment each month as I faced the fact that I wasn't pregnant. I had always been successful in life up to this point. I could count on one hand the number of times I had failed. I had no coping strategy for failing at something that I felt was so very natural and as basic as having a baby.

Lots of tests and a few years later, we were told that our choice was IVF or adoption. I had really had enough of dealing with the painful disappointment each month and felt I didn't have the emotional capacity to keep facing that disappointment through potential IVF fails.

I can vividly remember travelling home from a clinic appointment, driving around a roundabout and making the decision to adopt. It felt like a huge relief.

I thought I had gone through the most difficult period of my life.

It was during this time that I went from maths teacher to Youth Worker – I saw it as informal teaching and a great way to connect with kids.

We then embarked on the journey of adoption. The process for us was pretty straightforward and after two separate adoptions, we ended up with two lovely girls.

There is a myth in the adoption world that the younger the child, the less 'damaged' they would be. Well I can dispel that myth instantly!

This is why I became very involved in the world of adoption. I realised quite quickly that these children needed something much more than ordinary parenting. I needed to adapt. I embarked upon lots of learning about attachment and the effects of early trauma.

As they reached their teens, much of their behaviour was extreme. For me and my family however, life became extremely chaotic with police, social services, ambulances, hospitals, drugs and alcohol. I used to go to bed at night wondering if the next time I saw my daughter would be dead on a mortuary slab.

I was exhausted all the time and couldn't focus on anything. Work was too much. I would ask myself, "How can I support other adoptive families when I can't support my own?" I found that a very painful situation to be in.

I had to train myself into a different way of thinking. At bedtime I would tell myself that I could deal with the situation once I knew what was going on. So over time, I managed to switch off the 'what if' train of thought.

Another technique I used was to imagine a beautiful blue sky. Even on the cloudiest, darkest day I knew there was blue sky above me.

During the triumphs and failures of this time, one of the major lessons I learned was the need to look after myself.

We couldn't rely on support from social services as that was almost non-existent. Luckily, my parents supported me and my husband a great deal, giving us time out for us to recuperate.

If I reflect upon this time and how it affected me, I can see great benefits. I was able to learn a lot about myself. I decided to take a post-grad dramatherapy course. It was here I realised that up until now I had lived from my head. I didn't deal well with my emotions. This experientially taught course really helped me by connecting my head and my heart. Writing was helpful to express my journey. At that time I wrote a great deal about my process; how I was changing, what I was facing and how I was dealing with things.

I am grateful for this period in my life and the opportunities I had within it. This was a kick start into my journey of self-discovery and personal growth. Learning a new field of study, starting a new career path. If I hadn't adopted children then I would not have become an Attachment Therapist. I would not have met my wonderful, supportive colleagues who became very dear friends and actually saved my life. I am so grateful to this special group of women, who literally kept me alive with their love, compassion and non-judgmental support.

I was able to look at who I was and how I parented to be able to do my best for my girls.

A painful realisation I had was that I could not 'fix' my kids; I could not change them or their past. All I could do was change how I dealt with things, how I responded rather than reacted. They had to walk their own path and make their own mistakes. My role was to walk alongside them; helping them learn, keeping them safe and giving them a loving home to return to when they needed it.

I thought I had faced enough challenges for a while. It seems there was more self-discovery to be had.

The first was redundancy. It was the best thing that happened to me! I was very relived not to have to carry the emotional load of other adoptive families, while trying to hold my own.

The second was being diagnosed with chronic fatigue. I wasn't able to go out and find a job with the flexibility I needed, so I decided to take time out.

I knew meditation was helpful to me. As part of my new self-care regime I started going to the Bristol Buddhist Centre. I wasn't planning on becoming a Buddhist, I just wanted a quiet space and the opportunity to be away from the chaos of family life. A good mix of meditation and medication has seen me through these painful, difficult times.

Around this time my husband, Nigel started keeping bees. It was his hobby down at the bottom of the garden, nothing to do with me. I gradually became more interested and more involved.

While meditating one day I realised that I could make things out of beeswax. I felt as if I had birthed something. After more courses and learning I found a recipe, drew a little logo for myself and started making hand creams and lip balms. People were interested and I found myself attending craft fairs, until eventually, I started selling stock from a few shops around Bristol. I was able to work around my chronic fatigue, resting when needing to and working when I was able.

I very much saw it as a hobby; something to keep me occupied while I looked after my health and supported my girls.

My family life was still very chaotic and it took its toll, but I did not foresee what was about to happen.

I visited my sister in Australia. When I arrived back in the UK on Christmas Eve I was met at the airport by my husband with the words, "I don't want to be married anymore."

This came as a huge shock. I had always felt loved and very supported. We had been married for almost 30 years. We had grown together and had supported each other through many difficult times. We muddled through Christmas and my 50th birthday.

We decided to see if we could find a way to work things out, so signed up for some counselling. Unfortunately, there was too much of a gap to be bridged and we had gone too far apart to mend it. We separated in June 2016.

That was the final piece to my vision of what family life would be torn apart. I didn't know how I was going to survive this. I spent days, weeks and months crying; trying to figure out how to 'be' in the new world I found myself in.

Again, I felt I had no strategy to deal with the depth of the pain and anguish I felt. This is when I found support from my friends and my Buddhist practice. My Buddhist practice is the rock and foundation of my life. I know it is solid and I can rely on it to help and support me and to make sense of my life. Sitting in meditation has taught me I can turn towards the pain a bit at a time, so I don't get overwhelmed.

There was a part of me that thought we would get back together, so I stayed in our family home for some time. It slowly dawned on me that our reconciliation wasn't going to happen. I then made the decision to sell our family home. Again, a difficult and painful time but a necessary step to go through.

As a society we're sold the picture of what an ideal life should look like. In magazines, on TV, in the movies – 2.4 kids, two cars, a big house, a happy marriage and a successful career. It's everywhere, sometimes quite covert and we don't even realise we are buying in to it.

Here I am with a very different life to the one I was expecting or had planned. I now find myself living in my little cottage with a beekeeping business.

The Buddha and the bees are the main focus of my life now. I'm going through the process to become ordained and I will be given a Buddhist name. I'm feeling more 'me' than I have ever felt, although it certainly wasn't the 'me' I had plotted out for myself. I don't need a job, husband or children to measure my success. I don't need a man to make me complete or happy. It was me alone who created a new version of happiness and success.

With my health steadily improving and my business flourishing, life is starting to have more ease rather than struggle. There is now a great deal more blue sky above me and I look forward to new opportunities that come my way.

BEATRICE MARTIN

Bea's been interested in health for most of her life, particularly when a health crisis in her twenties propelled her into discovering more about complementary health, the subject of this chapter.

With jobs ranging from being on the Corporate Management Team of two general hospitals in her late twenties to now practising as a sound therapist, the wellbeing of others has often been at the core of her work.

She's had several articles on health and wellbeing published internationally both in magazines and online.

Based in the South West of England, she lives and works with her partner David as part of the duo Bards of Avalon. When they were both 50 they released their first album and have been working full-time as sound therapists since 2010. Like wandering minstrels, they also love to guide others around sacred sites with storytelling and live musical accompaniment.

They are currently writing a book about their adventures which they intend to have published in 2020.

Website: www.bardsofavalon.com

The University of Life

I didn't do sickness. Apart from a few minor childhood illnesses, I was a very robust child. I even won an award for never having a day off sick in my primary school. This earned me an additional award of being punched in the face by the school bully, but that's another story. Illness happened to other people, but not me. I was brought up to be self-reliant and resilient. That's how my family expected me to behave. I was the strong one; the caretaker, the fixer.

It was the early 80s. I'd left home, fulfilling a long-cherished dream of going to University, the first in my family to do so. My headmaster had told me many years previously that because my parents were foreigners and in low skill occupations, I didn't have the intellectual ability to progress very far with my education. However, here I was at Sheffield University having proved him wrong.

I'll never forget my first experience of Sheffield. It was pouring with rain and the air was filled with the pungent sweet and sour smell of the Henderson's Relish factory. It was grey, it was grim, but I absolutely loved it. The exciting vibrancy of the city was palpable and I felt like I'd come home.

It was a brilliant time to be a student. It seemed that everyone was either in a band or had a close link to band members, which was great as I could get into gigs for free. I was out most nights having a very active social life and was doing well on my University course, but my real education was about to come.

In my final year, I found myself in excruciating pain, feeling weak and vulnerable. The nausea and burning sensation in my stomach just wouldn't go away. The doctor's diagnosis was viral gastritis and said it would clear up quickly. In my inexperience and naivety, I'd taken aspirin not realising that it could make a stomach bleed and I ended up vomiting blood. I went back to the doctor, who gave me some drugs, but they didn't agree with me at all.

Any solid food I tried to eat would be swiftly brought back up. The only thing I could ingest was Complan, a powdered milk energy drink. By this stage, I was getting weaker; weight dropped off me and I felt utterly drained. I remember the shock as I was bathing myself and realising that my thighs were around half their former size. Only a few months previously I'd been able to dance the night away several nights a week. Now, to move from one end of a room to another was a monumental effort and I would collapse exhausted until I psyched myself up to move again.

I couldn't take pain killers as they would irritate the stomach lining. It felt like having an alien inside me constantly prodding my stomach with a burning hot poker.

My energy plummeted. I was so weak that I couldn't attend lectures. A kind fellow student lent me his lecture notes, although much of the time I felt too exhausted to read them.

There was one good thing about this time. I managed to miss one of the worst winters on record as I spent most of it in bed.

So many expectations had been placed on me by my family who now viewed me with disdain and contempt as I'd shattered their dreams. Not that going back to the family home in London was an option at this point. My parents had separated but were living under the same roof. My bedroom had gone so the sofa would be my bed. The atmosphere was toxic. I felt isolated and alone, yet my pride stopped me asking for their help.

Eventually, I was referred to a consultant who advised me to eat milk puddings, avoid citrus fruits and vegetables. Basically, anything with fibre. He decided I should have an endoscopy to investigate further.

I remember turning up at the hospital. I froze in horror. What on Earth was that? I saw what looked like a boa constrictor in a plastic tub of strong smelling disinfectant. It was the endoscope.

"Would you like Valium?" the assistant asked.

No, I wanted to be fully conscious during this process. I knew that a gagging reflex would be natural and I needed to have control. Being super self-reliant meant I'd gone on my own to hospital; I wanted to ensure I was clear-headed enough to travel home alone.

"Well, the good news is you don't have cancer, however the not so good news is that your entire digestive system looks like a Tetley tea bag." The assistant proceeded to tell me.

I strained to look at the grainy black and white screen showing the camera view of my insides. I had a morbid fascination with my insides on telly, yet still trying to suppress my natural instinct to gag.

The assistant went on to say, "Yes, your entire digestive system is pitted with ulcers and then you have two big duodenal ulcers. You must be in great pain."

To hear these words was like a soothing balm. The validation! For the first time in many months someone actually acknowledged what I was going through.

After the endoscopy, the consultant prescribed drugs which were designed to limit the amount of acid in the stomach, giving a chance for the body to repair and heal. That sounded fine in theory, however it made me even worse and affected my moods.

From being an active sociable person, I had become a recluse. I couldn't go out, eat or drink socially. I became acutely aware of how food and drink defined your life, particularly in my tribe. Friends dropped away. My housemates either ignored me or told me to pull myself together. That seemed to be the response from most people. I had literally become 'in-valid'.

I was extremely depressed. I didn't want to live anymore. What was the point of living if I was just existing? A young woman with supposedly a bright future ahead of her, yet spending 24/7 in excruciating pain with zero energy and nothing to live for. I felt very sorry for myself, as it had taken me so much to get to University. Now I didn't know if I could complete my degree and to be honest, I was past caring.

I had to go for another medical appointment. I needed to pace myself as my energy was so low. I'd stopped on a bench in a pedestrian precinct and was taking a few sips of water from a flask to help quell my pain. I don't know why, but I'd walked down that precinct countless times but had never noticed a shop. These were the days long before health food shops on the high streets. It was an independent herbalist and natural health shop. I'd never been there before and I never had a reason to go in, but something was drawing me inside.

I was guided to a rotating book stand, more specifically a thin volume on how to heal ulcers and ulcerative conditions naturally. I was intrigued. I had a quick leaf through the contents and was immediately struck by some of the suggestions given.

So, I bought it.

The book advocated a diet which was a complete contradiction of what the consultant had advised. It recommended herbs to heal the stomach lining and an initial juice diet. I asked myself, what did I have to lose?

I started off by taking the herbal remedy of slippery elm to soothe my digestive system and then juicing fruit and vegetables. Within a week, I felt much better. I was still in pain, but my energy was returning. I began to notice a sparkle in my eyes and a glossy sheen on my hair.

Emboldened by my progress, a few weeks later I tried to eat a salad. Bear in mind I had not eaten any solid foods for over six months. I felt like a baby moving onto solids for the first time. However, I'll never forget the day I ventured to eat a piece of toast with a bit of butter. I cried tears of relief! Finally, I could eat without vomiting!

The book was an opportunity to review my life and was a call to action. I had to face the truth that my classic student diet of drinking several cups of black coffee for breakfast, existing on takeaways and beans on toast, washed down with a lot of alcohol, wasn't great for my system. Before the illness, I was nearly 4 stone overweight. No wonder my poor body was screaming for attention.

This was the first time I'd really taken responsibility for my health. I'd been brought up to accept what doctors said was the absolute truth. Now I recognised my own authority about my health and wellbeing.

This was the catalyst for embarking on a lifelong journey exploring complementary health practices. The experience taught me a lot about listening; the importance of listening to our bodies and not solely relying on others' opinions. Listening is now at the core of my work as a sound therapist.

I was still in some pain when I took the exams and got my degree with a respectable grade. However, I feel I truly graduated when I regained my health thanks to the University of Life.

CHLOE BAYFIELD

My name is Chloe Bayfield and I live in Bristol with my husband and three girls. I love helping others, unravelling mess, the truth and making as many people as possible feel they are not alone.

My freelance work is varied but mostly involves words; including proofreading, copy editing and copy writing.

The Tiger Path

At 42, I am a Mother of three gorgeous girls. At the age of 23 I had my first baby and at that point my husband and I stepped onto two different paths. He became the breadwinner and I chose Motherhood. I have spent the last few years bouncing back from my path choice, exploring its ramifications and seeing my path from a different perspective. I knew I didn't have a career to go back to. I knew I was creating a large hole in my CV, so what did I think was going to happen?

Let's start by looking at the two paths. Jobs can be infinitely challenging and rewarding, or they can be a mind-numbing daily repetitive grind. If you remain within one career for a protracted period of time, while scaling the ladder, you are perceived increasingly to be an expert within your field. Naturally imbued with the relevant qualifications and skills. This is underlined and reinforced by achievements, references and qualifications. This is the career path.

The child-raising path is the same as the career path. The only part that is missing is the natural universal recognition of acquired skills. Parenting tests every skill set, every resource, every ounce of you, daily. You're learning crisis management, conflict resolution, facilitation, persuasion, motivation, inspiration and negotiation. The list is endless. Does the way in which you learn these valuable skills affect the value of the skill itself? I don't think so!

Parenting, for me, feels a lot like regularly re-evaluating and examining everything you've ever held to be true. Boring becomes a rare luxury. As we grow we gather beliefs, methods and habits. Once we have another person to care for we have to take another look at these. This is somebody else's life we're considering. Say we've chosen to be a vegetarian, who only works in female led companies, always wears stripes and only watches TV in GP waiting rooms. Are we happy that the principles upon which we have based these choices are ones we want to pass on to this human we're trying to raise?

The best bit is that you can evaluate your core beliefs, adjust life accordingly and be ready to move forward. A month, week or even an hour later something happens to make us need to think again. And that's only one child in one phase of their life. Trust me, what works for one will seldom work for them all!

This is sometimes soul destroying. It's not easy to question yourself so regularly. It can also be invigorating; I don't take anything for granted. I am very familiar with the concept that everything can, and regularly does, change entirely in 24 hours. If you need somebody with the ability to spin on a dime and change everything, somebody who can see things from other people's perspectives, a problem solver, then I'm your woman. You're not going to get that from all your job applicants who have more on their CV than I do and it's an invaluable skill.

While the paths themselves aren't that different, I think it would be fair to acknowledge that the environments in which they play out aren't identical. As a team leader in an insurance company, I was sometimes met with resistance and often with challenges. However, my team never went out of their way to either sabotage or entirely undermine my orders. If things went wrong there were two other managers above me to help; the buck didn't stop with me. The most significant differences though, were that I left them at 5pm and I didn't have to worry that my team leading decisions might affect the rest of their lives.

Although the paths are different, does that mean that the child-raising path's skills aren't as valuable? Aren't transferable? I personally believe that the skills learnt while raising children are priceless. I think it's about time they were recognised as such.

My role as a Mother is exhausting. I work 12-hour days and regularly pull all-nighters. My bosses are unforgiving, unrealistic and have anger issues. I don't get holidays, I can't take time off sick, I can't quit and I don't get paid.

I am a Mother to three mind-bendingly brilliant and breathtakingly infuriating girls and my job is the single most rewarding thing I have ever done.

I'm not saying my life is harder than anybody else's and I'm not saying that I want gratitude or payment. I am saying that I believe my job amounts to more than the gaping hole it's left on my CV.

Last year all three girls were fully settled in full-time education and various medical challenges had calmed down. It was time to go back to work. I was excited! I could talk to adults again, finish sentences - in fact, finish anything – uninterrupted and I couldn't wait! I sat down to write my CV... at least I tried. As I stared at that blank piece of paper, I realised I had somehow managed to have NO experience despite having experienced EVERYTHING! It felt like running into a brick wall. It was as if the last 17 years of life had been stolen from me in an instant. Had I really done nothing? Could that be right? I moaned about being tired, a lot. How could I always be so very tired if I had done nothing?

Or maybe it wasn't that I had done nothing, perhaps it was that what I had done counted for nothing? I had raised three children, they were alive, reasonably well fed and didn't seem to be psychopaths. Job done, your children and society thanks you, goodnight! If that were so, then I would surely find myself, developmentally speaking, in the same place as when I left work to have children? That seemed to be what my CV was implying.

Then I started looking over my parenting career from a different angle. Had I done nothing? Or had I run a house, been the primary caregiver to three children and helped my husband? To say that in doing so I learnt nothing would imply I held some passive role in our lives. Now that definitely doesn't sound right. In our home, I'm the project manager, the coach, the nurse and the negotiator on any given day. Take another snapshot and you'll find me playing researcher, advocate and teacher.

These skills weren't taught to me in a comfortable out of town two-day training seminar with a lovely cooked lunch. I didn't have the chance to read the theory, do some practice role-plays and then go back over the bits I hadn't fully understood. I learnt these skills in the moment, on the day, after no sleep. I then had to get good at them, fast! Not only that, my team was pretty hostile.

Imagine being a team leader to a team who not only refuse to do what you ask, they also frequently tell you that you don't know what you're doing. Oh and by the way - they could do it better! Picture days where you spend hours making phone calls and fighting battles for one of your colleagues, only to be told that they didn't ask you to do it and that they strongly suspect you've done it wrong. Imagine working for bosses who occasionally throw up on you or demand that you don't go to the toilet alone!

I have indeed learnt extremely useful skills during my time as a Mother and it occurred to me that my CV, with its gaping hole of experience, was wrong. I felt undervalued, or devalued. So I decided to fix it by recognising my true skills and worth; showing that to the world as my experience and expertise.

To help other women I have developed a method called The Tiger Path. The Tiger Path is a programme that parents work through to translate the highs and lows of parenting into concrete employable skills. I did a lot of market research and found a lot of people who loved the idea and wanted to join. This is not without its challenges.

I called my programme The Tiger Path because you earn your parenting stripes. We all walk our own parenting path, earning slightly different stripes depending on the journey. I also feel that tigers are opponents that you'd do well not to underestimate in a fight. It's only happened a small handful of times, but if I have to fight for my girls then I will and that power is stronger than anything else I've ever known.

My value only surfaced when I stopped looking to others to find it. Parenting left me with a lot of doubt and not much self-esteem. Society didn't seem to care about all my hard work and the job market didn't seem interested in what I had to offer. But I knew I had learnt so much. I then noticed I was having the same conversations with friends. Brilliant women with huge value, who either didn't recognise it in themselves, couldn't find work, or both. I knew something had to be done.

In addition to helping others to walk the Tiger Path, I am freelancing for women, often mothers, running their own businesses. This is really enjoyable and is highly compatible with my family life. Women don't realise how amazing they are. We are frequently so overwhelmed that many I meet have lost sight of the vision and can't see the path that's quite often right there, hidden amongst the firefighting.

The bottom line for me is I now know I have value and I very much want to help others to find theirs.

CLAIRE BLACK

Claire Black is a leading Break-up and Divorce Coach. Through her unique Metamorphosis coaching programme, she offers empathetic, bespoke coaching to support individuals through break-up, so that they can create new and vibrant lives. She is a Master NLP Practitioner, divorcee and Mum to two teenage boys.

In a former life she was a lawyer in London. She is the author of "From Crisis to Confidence; how to recover from a sudden break-up or divorce", due out early 2020.

Connect with Claire:

Website: www.claireblackcoaching.com

LinkedIn: https://www.linkedin.com/in/claire-black-divorce-coach/

Facebook: https://www.facebook.com/ClaireBlackDivorceCoaching/

Twitter: https://twitter.com/CBDivorceCoach

Bouncing Back from a Sudden Separation

On 25 March 2008, my world as I knew it crashed down around me, making me question everything I thought was true.

I was 35, married with two boys aged 3 and 1. I had recently gone back to work as a solicitor after maternity leave and my husband had a successful career working in IT strategy. We lived in a lovely, suburban house in a leafy part of Bristol. We were in the middle of planning an extension to give us a bigger, more open-plan living space; perfect for a growing family.

All sounds wonderful, doesn't it? Only that afternoon, I had been at the gym with a friend. I was talking about my family and how my husband was a great dad. How I looked forward to him coming home in the evening so that I could take my eyes off our toddlers for a while.

And then it happened. As we watched Holby City I thought he seemed a bit quiet and withdrawn, so I asked him if he was OK. He said two sentences that changed the course of my life forever.

"No, not really. I've been seeing someone else".

He might have said more, but that's all I remember. I do remember my first reaction was to do that thing that I thought people only did in movies – I slid down the wall and ended up sitting on the floor, in a foetal position cradling my knees. I didn't know what to do or what to say, so I did the first thing that came into my head. I went next door. I figured if I went out, he couldn't leave because the children were asleep upstairs.

My neighbours later told me that when I had knocked on their door my expression, my inability to speak and the total lack of any colour in my face had scared them. They thought something had happened to one of the children and they were actually relieved when I finally managed to blurt out what had just happened.

When I walked back through the door an hour or so later, his bag was waiting in the hall and he left then; to where I didn't know. I had not prepared for this moment and I had not seen it coming. I hadn't realised he was unhappy. Looking back, I went into shock. I couldn't think clearly at all. I felt as though I had been run over by a train.

The first few weeks after that are still a blur. I very quickly lost 2 stone, dropping from a size 12 to a 6-8. I couldn't eat, I felt sick and I developed IBS-type symptoms. I couldn't concentrate and I didn't believe what was happening. For a while, I believed he would come home. Well-meaning friends told me that he would 'see sense', that he would 'realise what a mistake he was making', but he didn't do any of those things. It became clear over the next few weeks that this was permanent.

For the first time in my life, I didn't know what the future looked like. The future I thought I had was no longer an option and all I could see was uncertainty. I struggled with the emotional turmoil – one minute I might be crying, the next I would feel insanely angry and the next lonely and sad. I felt confused and overwhelmed, but most of all, scared. I had no idea whether I would be able to stay in my house, whether my husband would be there for the children, or how I would manage financially.

I also began to question my own worth. Had this happened because I was a bad wife? Had I neglected my husband and spent too much energy on our children? If I was slimmer/funnier/sexier – would that have made a difference? Questions swirled around my head, all ultimately leading me to question whether I was good enough.

As I write this chapter nearly 12 years on, I am remarried and running my own business, coaching others to help them create new lives after divorce or separation.

As I reflect on what it was that enabled me to bounce back, at the core of it is my belief that it is not what happens to you that makes the difference – it is what you do with what happens to you. You always have choices about how you react. What you do, and those choices can change your life.

I decided very early on that I wanted to swim, not sink. I didn't want my divorce to define me and I wanted to be happy again. I was determined that it wasn't going to beat me! It was the choices I made after my husband left that made me the person I am today.

Dignity at all times

'Dignity at all times' and 'plaster on a smile' became my mantras. I had realised that I felt better when I got up, showered and made a bit of an effort. The days when I hung about the house in my tracksuit or pyjamas were the worst.

I didn't know then about the correlation between how you stand and how you feel, or that smiling releases endorphins into the bloodstream. I hadn't yet done lots of reading about the power of mantras and affirmations. I just knew that it made me feel stronger when I wore nice clothes, put on make-up and a smile and reminded myself to be dignified. Especially when I had to see my husband. 'Dignity at all times' helped me maintain my composure when it might otherwise have slipped.

I would be lying if I didn't admit that, in the early days, I also felt that it might make my husband realise what he was missing – this composed, well-dressed woman who was his wife. It didn't have that effect, but it did mean that I began to feel stronger and more confident. It also means that 12 years on, I feel hugely proud of my behaviour.

Find the upside

I didn't realise until my husband left me what an optimist I am at heart.

I tried to find the 'upside' to everything, almost like it was a challenge. I always knew I had good friends and I soon saw just how amazing they were. As one person left, it gave me the space to make new friends whom I never would have met otherwise. I learnt how to dance and I bought a road bike – because now I could. I had time that I had not had before. I could eat beans on toast with the children if I wanted. I could cook with ginger (which my husband hated!). On weekends when the children were with him, I could visit friends and go to parties. I could go out with my friends without having to check with anyone else (other than the babysitter). I could make plans that were just for me.

I know some of my friends and family found it surprising that I didn't stay angry for long; how I didn't want to punish my husband for what he had done. That isn't to say that I wasn't angry at all; I was, but I could see the damage it would do to me. For me, staying angry was pointless. All it meant was that I would be letting what had happened define who I was.

Finding the upside helped me to turn around my angry feelings and focus on what was good in my life. It gave me hope.

Choice and control

I had a lightbulb moment when I realised that I always had choices, then another when I saw that I could choose to let go of things I couldn't control. The first big test of this was when my husband introduced the children to his girlfriend.

Although it was hard imagining them off having fun with them, I knew that I couldn't control what he did in his time with the children. I realised that trying to do so would only end in frustration, anger and conflict.

I chose instead to take a long-term view. I knew what I wanted our children to feel on their wedding days. I had been to friends' weddings where the divorced parents of the bride or groom couldn't sit together, or even be in the same room. I didn't want that for our children – at least not as a result of any of my choices. I want our children not to even think about us when they are making choices about top tables. I want them to know that we can sit together; that we are both proud of the young men they have become. I want them to know that whatever happens, we are their parents and that we both love them.

I have rewritten the story of my sudden separation. I could tell a story of a terrible night when my world fell apart. How I was cruelly and brutally left by the man who had promised to love me until death us do part. Instead, I choose to tell a different story. My story tells the strength of one woman. One who found resilience and strength through adversity. One who can handle anything that life might throw at her. One who redefined herself and created a new life for herself and her children.

One woman who knows that she is good enough.

DANNY LLOYD

A former construction coordinator/design engineer.

I have Anti Phospholipid Syndrome (APS), which caused two strokes, kidney damage & adrenal insufficiency.

Bodybuilding's played a huge part in my life. I've practiced jujitsu, judo and road cycling. I became a yoga practitioner which was the start of my self-discovery journey. The greatest and most noticeable changes however have come from Tai Chi practice.

I'm a founding member of 'The Brain Injury Cafe Bristol' a peer group for anyone affected by a brain injury.

I've become a 'Stroke Ambassador' for the Stroke Association & spoke about my experiences at the international congress for APS in Manchester.

Facebook: The Reset Button

Facebook: The Brain Injury Cafe Bristol

Instagram: The.Reset.Button

Email: dlloydy1973@gmail.com

My Stroke Of Luck

Finding the authentic, real me.

Life: Part One

Through playing rugby at school I started weight training, which later led to Bodybuilding. As I improved, I entered an amateur bodybuilding contest. This was a massive decision for me, as I had lacked confidence and suffered from anxiety that started in my mid-teens. How I looked then did not match how I felt.

I was hospitalised late in 1995 when I was first diagnosed with Antiphospholipid Syndrome (APS), also known as Hughes Syndrome or more commonly 'sticky blood'. At the time, it was a bolt from the blue. I later discovered I had suffered mini strokes and kidney damage which changed the direction of my life.

Life: Part Two

Early on New Year's Day 2013 around 5am, I collapsed in the bathroom at home. I tried to crawl back to bed but kept collapsing onto my face. An ambulance was called and I was admitted to the hospital through the emergency department.

It transpired that the APS I have, which had been generally well managed since 1995 had become the much feared Catastrophic variant. This is extremely rare, having a 50% mortality rate and affecting less than 1% of those with an APS diagnosis.

I had experienced a spontaneous midline cerebellar haemorrhage, or haemorrhagic stroke. Then very quickly afterwards, I suffered kidney and adrenal infarction, resulting in chronic kidney disease & adrenal insufficiency. Additionally, I contracted two brain conditions, hydrocephalus & then ventriculitis (an infection similar to meningitis).

The Road to Recovery

Initially I was in the Intensive Treatment Unit and placed into an induced coma to rest my failing body. My kidneys had begun failing and it became a medical balancing act for those treating me. This worsened with the brain condition/infection. I received blood plasma transfusions as part of the treatment; my records state I had 20 in total.

Once I was out of the acute phase of treatment, I started to realise the magnitude of what had happened to me and the position I was now in.

Due to the stroke I had to relearn things I had taken for granted since childhood. These included speaking, as I now slurred, mumbled and couldn't form words properly. I was unable to sit unsupported as I had no natural balance. I regularly fell out of chairs and out of bed. I dislocated my fingers, suffered numerous cuts and bruises and grazed my head and face several times due to falling. I couldn't sit up unassisted, get out of bed, use the toilet, wash, dress, drink from a cup or eat without help. The first time I was allowed to 'sit out' in a chair I had to wear a seatbelt!

Progress

Rehabilitation started, after around 3 months of me being an inpatient. I expected to be working in a gym environment, however I was given a sponge rugby ball to pass around my waist while sitting up unassisted. I couldn't do it! I knew I had to learn these things if I was to progress and get home. I worked hard at whatever I was given to do.

Standing from a sitting position was particularly difficult and frustrated me. I consider myself fortunate as I did not lose obvious cognitive function. Early on, I felt terrified of falling and being as stuck as I was at that point.

My early rehab progressed and my task now was to relearn how to walk. I had to wear a safety belt with handles for my protection, which I hated! I persisted and gradually got better at it. In April, talk began of a place becoming available at the nearby residential Brain Injury Rehabilitation Unit. I was very keen to move to the unit as places at B.I.R.U. are limited.

A meeting was arranged with a lead consultant from the unit, who came to speak with and assess me. I remember begging him, in tears, to give me a chance to get a life back worth having. I feared being trapped in a body, which did not feel like mine anymore and worse was the feeling of being unable to control it.

I was offered a place and I moved over in late April 2013. After I settled in a timetable was agreed, which covered the areas that I needed therapy in. These included physiotherapy, neuropsychology, speech therapy and occupational health.

I remained at the Unit for 2 months, finally being discharged at the end of June 2013. By then, I had spent 6 months in total in hospitals.

The Next Chapter

Once I was home, I soon realised how badly affected I actually was. I couldn't move around my home safely, feed myself, wash or dress. I felt angry and frustrated as I had always been fiercely independent and did not like receiving help from anyone, despite very obviously needing it.

Swimming soon became my focus, as I felt protected from the constant fear of falling when I was in the water. I later progressed to walking on a treadmill, then a gym exercise bike. Eventually I committed to a weekly indoor cycling (spinning) class.

Recovery – A Physical and Mental Process

I came to realise that awareness was the key to so many things. Essentially, awareness is unforced attention that is without thought. It is simply paying relaxed attention to oneself.

By way of example, after my stroke my left hand was clawed. I tried physically stretching, strengthening and doing other therapeutic exercises which didn't really help. It was suggested that I simply be more aware of it by paying relaxed attention, rather than focusing directly on it. I tried, I persevered and it worked.

Being physically active and health conscious before this whole period, I believe, has allowed me to get a good standard of life back.

I complained in hospital that, "I'd looked after myself, ate well, kept fit and yet this still happened to me so what was the point?" I remember a nurse saying to me, "Have you ever thought you might not be here if you hadn't?"

I now know that recovery takes effort. People seek help at the first opportunity, choosing the easy option. Essentially by doing this, they are denying themselves the opportunity to find out what they are capable of. Taking responsibility, I believe, cultivates inner strength, resilience and it develops the will.

My philosophy of life is that we can all learn from our difficulties. How, if we work to overcome them, they will reveal our true character. Our difficulties give us an opportunity to discover our true capabilities and our authentic self.

Tragedy awakens a person to what really matters. It shifts perspective and gives clarity...all in that single moment. I see it as an opportunity to start again, to find and live your purpose. I felt my Reset Button was pressed and I had the chance to do things differently.

Life can, and does, change in an instant. Along my journey I have realised how disability and in particular brain injury, together with other 'hidden illnesses' are generally viewed by the public. Either it's believed to be a complete dramatic miracle case or the vegetative state scenario. The reality is that 99% of people with a brain injury are somewhere between the ends of this spectrum.

I choose to focus on the things I can do and do not waste my time on what I can't. Debilitating events in my life have led me to self-awareness through learning and consistent practice. I pay attention to what I am doing far more now, I live in the present moment and I realise I only have control over my own thoughts, actions and behaviour.

I'm grateful for everything because of my experience and do my best to live with that outlook. I love my life. It really is a gift and one we all take for granted.

The Way Forward

The condition (APS) has no cure, but it is treatable. APS put a stop to my bodybuilding, just as it was getting going. I have never given up maintaining a healthy lifestyle and keeping fit despite difficulties.

A massive turning point in my rehabilitation and health generally came from starting Tai Chi. I was far from impressed and I remember saying that, "No way was I doing exercise for old people", but I persevered.

The progress and difference in my day to day ability through consistent practice since starting has been unbelievable.

When I first started, I had to stand with my back against a wall, as I couldn't stand upright unsupported without falling. I also experienced unexplained violent twitches that had started in the hospital and no one could explain what they were.

Six years on and I have learned parts of tai chi forms, the twitching has all but stopped and I have learned so much about myself.

The Future

I realise if I can survive what I did and live the rewarding life I now do despite my difficulties, I can do pretty much anything I apply myself to.

Early on in my recovery I decided I had to give something back to society when I was able to. I consider fully accepting my situation has been key to my moving forward. I remain focused on the things I can do and I do not waste my time on things that I can't. Occasionally, I look back and reflect on how far I've come with pride.

DEB JAMES

At 61, Deb is finally in a place, with the help she needs, to live her life - her way. Deb has studied holistic therapies and always helps the close circle that she now counts as family. She is on a path to help more people, putting to good use her lived experience of the past that she has finally come to terms with. Deb lives in Bristol with her two cats Skidoo and Lights. She loves a variety of hobbies including crochet and spending time with friends.

Getting It Right

I'm approaching 61, not knowing what the years in front of me are going to bring. However, I sure know where I have been and to tell you the truth, I really don't know how I am still here to tell any kind of story. There have been times I just wanted to throw the towel in, just to get some peace from the torment of living in a body and mind that was out of balance. I would lose sight of hope that things would ever get better, I would think that my future would just be my past repeating itself.

The 22nd February 2016 was the day my mother passed. She had 'tarred and scarred' me from the beginning of my life until the end of hers. I don't know why she could never see the spirit I really was until it was too late, for the both of us. For some reason I was always the Devil's daughter to her, no matter how I tried to show her I wasn't. As the saying goes, 'They never remember the good you do only the bad,' and this had been the way it was for me from the age of three. Between the ages of one and three I had been shipped off to live with my grandparents, while she worked at B.O.C.

While living with my grandparents, they were my family. In fact on one occasion a neighbour knocked and told Nan there was a call for her. She told me that my mother was coming to see me and I remember thinking, "What is a mother?" When she arrived she was all over me, which I wasn't used to and I squirmed to get away. I believe the reason for the visit was due to a miscarriage that she had between me and my younger sister.

My sister was born in March 1962. The first I knew was when I was woken up during the night to be told I would be moving. The room was in darkness except for the glass over the door where the light came in. I could sense that my Nan was upset as she told me that I would be leaving her to go and live with my parents and my new sister. After she went, I was left back in the darkness, scared and alone. Not sure what was going to happen next.

I was soon to learn my life was going to change big time and not for the better once I returned to my parents. Up to this point I didn't know anything about being chastised, being segregated, slapped or shouted at. I also learned that I could fly, as I was thrown in temper across the room.

The brainwashing started too, as I learned from my mother that I was a naughty, bad child or the Devil's daughter.

The only time I remember anyone trying to stand up for me was on a train trip to Weymouth. My Aunties Val and Marie asked my mother why she always picked on me. This didn't go down well. My mother sulked for the rest of the day and ignored me, putting all of her attention on my sister.

In the early days, the treatment I received was not so bad when Dad was around. Dad wasn't an easy man. He had a hard upbringing himself, but his style of parenting was far different from Mum's. In so many ways, I am who I am today more because of him.

When I was about eight, I had to attend Child Guidance and at the time I didn't know what it was. Mum would take me out of school and we would travel to the centre at Monks Park Avenue by bus. It was on one such occasion I started to ask questions as to why I was being taken out of school and no one else was. My mother replied by telling me I had to see a psychiatrist. "What's a Psychiatrist?" I asked. She replied by telling me it was someone who mad people see. It wasn't long after this that the visits stopped and we were moving. I often wonder if that was because Mum was told I wasn't the problem, but she was.

It was also around this age my younger sister had got increasingly adept at getting me into trouble, either by telling tales or starting a fight. The lying came a little after. She learned quickly not to start in front of Mum with her spitefulness, as she would be told off along with me. Instead she would do it when Mum was in the kitchen and we were in the living room. She would pinch me and pull my hair until I retaliated. She would then get herself into a position that I could get to her and start screaming. My mother would knock me for six and I would get sent to the bedroom. I soon learned there was no point telling Mum about her behaviour towards me. I was either called a liar or told to ignore her – which was easier said than done. I thought of my sister as a crafty fox.

By the time I was 11 I didn't want to live anymore and thoughts of self-harm entered into my mind. I thought about stepping out in front of a lorry or bus to end it - but what if I did not die and had to live with even more pain? At 12 due to my behaviour at school I was back at Child Guidance, where I was prescribed 10mg of Valium twice a day. I didn't like the way they made me feel, I was doped up all day at school and when it came to bedtime I would spend most of the night awake. I complained to my mother about the effects of the drug, which fell on deaf ears and she ensured I took my daily dose. By 13 I had taken my first overdose, which was treated by doctors and family like an everyday thing.

Before I reached the age of 18 I was thrown out of the house due to my sister's lies. I got into a fight with my father for using the word sprog in front of him and he treated it like the worst swear word in the dictionary. He told me to go to my room, I refused to go and he chased me up the stairs, followed my mother. He pinned me down on my bed and was going to burn me on the face with the lighted cigarette in his mouth. I manage to break my right arm free from his grasp by digging my nails into the back of his neck. When he jerked back with pain, I grabbed the cigarette, throwing it into the corner of the bedroom. With that he ordered Mum, who had stood in the doorway, to get the lighted cigarette. She was like a rabbit in headlights and just stood there, so he got up and went to retrieve it for himself. This gave me the chance to escape, after which Dad opened my bedroom window and started to throw out my things. I needed to be out of it.

That night I slept rough in the women's toilet at the top of Sturminster Road and the next morning I went back home. Dad refused me entrance due to my sister claiming that every time my parents went out I would beat her up - which was totally untrue. If either one of my parents thought about it, they would realise I was either out or working overtime. Dad called me a liar and told me I was no longer welcome in the house. I was homeless, hurt and alone.

Life from there was all downhill. With nowhere to go I first moved in with a friend of my uncle's in Hartcliffe, into what could be called a life of chaos and self-destruction. I was abused by one of my uncle's best friends. I never mentioned this to anyone, because I did not think anyone would believe me. I also lost my job. There were more nights sleeping anywhere I could find, sometimes on stairs in blocks of flats in Hartcliffe. I also fell into hanging around with the wrong crowds, taking drugs and stealing cars to sleep in, once I was shown how.

By 19 I was doing my first term in Borstal (youth detention centre). Once I came home things were a little better for a while. I stayed with my Uncle Ray and his girlfriend. It was whilst I was there I met Ann, who lived in the corner of the square. We became friends and in the end I went and lived with her. Ann was like a mother to me in so many ways. It was while I was staying with her that I met my husband and went to live with him and his parents. That wasn't to last, like most things in my life. When I left him, I went back to live with Ann for a while, until my in-laws pressured me to leave Keynsham. This is when I went to stay in a girl's hostel in St. Pauls, with all the problems that came with living in an inner city red-light district.

Even after I had my daughter in 1982 and got my own place things didn't get any better. I used to joke that my middle name should have been "Trouble," because if there was any going around I would find it and suffer the consequences!

The fact was, I was alone. Like an urchin wishing to belong to a family that I was not good enough for, no matter how many times I was there for them in their hour of need. In December 1988, I had to go into hospital for a cone biopsy, which required me to have several units of blood. It wasn't until December 2012 that I found out that I had been living with Hepatitis C for all those years. It affected me both mentally and physically, making it very difficult for me to care for myself let alone my daughter. I had to regularly ask social services for support with her care, after I had been refused help by my mother. In 1997 asking them for help turned out to be the biggest mistake of my life.

The sicker I got the more indifferent my family got about my mental illness and I was excluded. The treatment I received in childhood worsened, to the point that in 2010 my mother refused to have anything to do with me, due to my sister and my daughter's lies. She told me I was dead to her.

At my uncle's wake in May 2014 I overheard my family telling other family members lies. That it wasn't them who didn't want to know me, but me who didn't want to know them. I did not think it was appropriate at the time to say anything, due to the circumstances and the statement being so untrue, so left it until the June to ring her.

I was coming to the end of my treatment to clear the HCV when we started to speak again. To my surprise once I contacted my Mum she asked if she could come over to see me, which she did. We talked and for the first time I had a mother. She not only listened to what I had to say, but also asked questions about my sister and daughter's claims against me, their lies being her reason for not talking to me from 2010. For the first time she saw me for who I really am. Before she passed she wanted to undo the wrong she had done in 2012, when she changed her Will so that the majority of the estate went to my sister.

My sister did not comply with Mum's last wishes to get her solicitor to visit so that the Will could be changed. She also did not keep her promise to our mother that I would never see the Will of 2012, even though she maintained all the way through probate to both sides of our family that she was doing her best to comply.

I believe that God pays debts (karma), my life has shown me that much. It is coming up to the fourth anniversary of Mum's passing. I am trying to rebuild my life into the life that I always wanted but never felt I deserved due to the way my family treated me. I realise that I'm not as bad as I was made out to be and that what other people think of me, because of the story they have been told, is not important. What is important is how the people in my life now treat me. When crisis hits, it's all about taking one day at a time or even one second if life gets that bad. One thing I know for sure is that nothing stays the same. As the seasons change so does everything else, if you are willing to let go of the pain and hurt and start anew. As I go into my 61st year, I think I am finally getting it right.

JEMMA BARTHOLOMEW

Jemma Bartholomew lives with her dog Boris, a gorgeous Lab/Basset cross. She grew up in Sussex but has lived as an adult in Wales, Scotland, Spain, London and Azerbaijan, before moving to Bath. She has travelled extensively and is multi-lingual.

She spent nearly 18 years working on the commercial side of multi-billion dollar international oil and gas developments, but has not been able to work properly for nearly 10 years due to chronic ill health. She is currently working hard on regaining her health, and is considering various ideas and options for her future.

If You're Going Through Hell, Keep Going

It was coming up to midnight when the men woke us up and asked us, two solo ladies in their early-thirties, what we were doing camping near the Iranian border in Azerbaijan. Umm, trying to sleep?

And so begins the story of how I was once questioned by the ex-KGB military police whilst wearing my pyjamas. You couldn't make it up. Working on international oil projects and based in Azerbaijan for 5 years in the early noughties, going exploring and camping at the weekend was a perfectly normal thing to do. I worked very hard and I travelled constantly. My life was busy and exciting and full of adventure.

Roll forward a few years and life was very different. At this time, I was experiencing severe frozen shoulder pain that was beyond excruciating. Together with tennis elbow, underlying chronic Repetitive Strain Injury (RSI) pain (which by then I'd had for several years), and burning neuropathic pain, my right hand and arm were basically non-functional. Just getting dressed was a challenge; I had given up on wearing a bra. Driving was a distant memory. Cooking for me was a microwave meal that I could eat with only a fork.

This went on for two years.

Two long, hard years of living alone, effectively disabled but without a disability, and in constant pain. Constant, never-ending burning pain. I would think about the carefree fun I used to have and be amazed how that used to be me. What happened to that adventurous girl whose life force couldn't be contained?

I was crushed.

I had private healthcare, but even with that, it took two years of the doctors failing to resolve the shoulder problem before they finally gave in to my begging and did elbow surgery.

Instant relief. How many people can come around from an anaesthetic and be immediately in less pain than they'd been in for two years?

Hallelujah!

I could move my shoulder and begin rehabilitation. I was taking significantly less painkillers, I got my lovely dog and met my lovely boyfriend. I still had massive limitations and ongoing problems with chronic pain, but it was all going so well and I was slowly recovering.

And then I got chronic fatigue.

I couldn't believe it. After a year of relative respite, I was back to rock bottom. I still couldn't drive, but now I couldn't walk anywhere either.

It was s**t. Utterly, utterly s**t. I felt 90. Not in so much pain as before, but tired, oh so tired. And utterly miserable. Was this it? Was this going to be the rest of my life?

Chronic pain, chronic fatigue, depression. This was not how I thought my forties were going to play out. This was not part of my plan. This was not 'me', but it was my life.

Winston Churchill once said "If you're going through hell, keep going." That really resonates for me.

When I was at my absolute lowest, a relatively new acquaintance gave me the single most important piece of information of my life: "Have you heard of The Chrysalis Effect? If you do nothing else in the next week, promise me you'll look at their website."

I hadn't heard of them, but I did look at their website.

Oh my goodness!

In an internet world where EVERYTHING about chronic fatigue is doom and gloom, saying "You will be like this forever", The Chrysalis Effect were offering a structured recovery programme, designed by people who themselves had suffered with and recovered from chronic pain and fatigue. As a not-for-profit and recognising that many people in this position are on restricted incomes, the basic course, delivered online via weekly modules and membership of the positive Facebook support group, was only £24/month.

I couldn't sign up quick enough, and I'm so glad I did.

Over the 9 months of the programme I learned all about the myriad causes of chronic fatigue. I started understanding what was happening to my mind and body. The programme gave me many suggestions, ideas and steps to aid recovery.

I knew my diet wasn't great (feeling so rubbish does that to you, I comfort ate my way through life), so signed up to see a nutritionist/naturopath, who had herself recovered from fatigue. I embraced everything she suggested. At the bi-annual Recoverer's Day, I sat in a roomful of approx. 100 people, many of whom had recovered. From wheelchair bound to running half marathons. From bed to world-championship glory.

It was SO inspiring.

I envisaged one of those big red thermometers that people use if they're raising money for a new church roof - except it represented my recovery. I could see a way forward: I knew that if I made lots of small changes, they would contribute a bit here and a bit there. If I made some pretty big changes, it would increase by chunks rather than just small steps. But there had to be something else. Something that would be transformative and get me 50% of my energy back in one stroke.

I had NO IDEA what that was, but I knew it would be *something*.

My lovely reflexologist Siân invited me on a retreat she was organising. I'd not been on a retreat before. I felt a little out of my comfort zone but was definitely in the frame of mind for trying anything that might help. Her friend Sybil is a Spiritual Healer and was offering treatments. What the hell, why not? I thought. Nothing ventured nothing gained.

It was *transformative*.

The metaphorical cork burst and in unstoppable waves, the emotion came pouring out of me. I was not a mother. I was never going to be a mother. I was 45 and with no hope of ever being a mother. I was devastated. I had always wanted to be a mother but as I went through my thirties with increasing ill health and an ever higher number of hideous first dates stacking up behind me, I thought I had reconciled with not becoming a mother. When I met my boyfriend aged 43, I actually said 'getting pregnant would be a disaster' and had a coil fitted.

That was the beginning of my chronic fatigue.

My body HATED the coil, my mind hated it even more – together they were SCREAMING at me to take it out and try for a child, but the message got lost in translation. Childlessness was SO painful that my brain had, in order to protect me from the emotional pain, redirected it towards fatigue and physical pain instead.

Within months of the big revelation, I had started to get some energy back. The pain had reduced to the point that I could drive and I had really turned a corner. Regaining my full health and fitness continues to be a bigger challenge, but I'm getting there. Health is my number one priority and I have a range of things that I do daily, weekly and monthly that support my health.

But the story doesn't quite end there, and no, there is no miracle baby. Two and a half years on from the big revelation, aged 47 and following a protracted debate with my boyfriend about trying IVF with a donor egg, I've acknowledged that I am childless and I'm going through the very real grieving process for the children I will not have.

It's brutal and painful and every day there are unexpected triggers. Even casually flicking through a Hello magazine at the hairdressers is a physical assault, with all those pregnancy bumps and new baby photo shoots. I don't hate babies – I love them – I'm just not going to have my own and that's heart breaking.

I turned once again to the internet and found Gateway Women, a support group for women who are Childless Not By Choice. It's relatively early days but already I have found it SO helpful. I understand that my situation today reflects the unintended consequence of choices I made when I was younger. Choices that have enriched my life with joy, friendship and experiences I will treasure for the rest of my life, including *that* nocturnal encounter with the KGB.

Now, rather than burying this, it is out in the open and I am acquiring the tools to work through it. After nearly a decade-long "health hiatus", I can finally start to think and tentatively plan how I might enrich the second half of my life as much as I did the first, even if it's not quite how I imagined.

I am not entirely sure what my journey will be yet, but it sure as hell is going to be AWESOME.

Things I do to support my health:

Daily:

Good diet, nutrition, good quality supplements., no caffeine or alcohol

Fresh air, nature, walk my dog

Moisturise my body and feet, as well as my face

Afternoon naps, in bed by 10pm, general 'pacing'

Bounce on my mini-trampoline

Laugh

Be honest with myself and assertive with others about what I can/can't do

Try to tone down my perfectionist behaviours

Weekly:

Swimming

Meditation

Proper work outs, with a personal trainer or at home

Counsellor, grief work, dealing with the difficult emotional stuff

Network chiropractor

Monthly:

Reflexology

Osteopath

Gong sound bath (if you've never tried this, it's HEAVEN!)

Other things I did that helped:

Had my coil removed

Reiki

Heavy Metal detox, including removal of mercury fillings

Dr Alan Gordon 'tms wiki' online pain recovery programme

PAMELA ROSE

Pamela Rose is a believer in the power of positivity and (so her mum tells her) has been a 'glass half full' person since she was a toddler. This, coupled with an ever-increasing desire to help people improve their lives, lead to Pamela leaving a corporate career of 30+ years to retrain as a Wellness Coach.

Pamela derives huge satisfaction from helping people work towards their health or lifestyle goals. Her personal recovery story from ME/Chronic Fatigue Syndrome has particularly drawn her to inspire and help those who are tackling their own recoveries.

Originally from Glasgow, Pamela now lives in Bristol with her husband Pete and definitely has the travel bug with a house in Murcia, Spain and a passion for travelling in the Far East.

Pamela Works with clients locally in Bristol, but also throughout the UK and overseas. You can reach her at:

Website: www.pamelarose.co.uk

Email: info@pamelarose.co.uk

Facebook: www.facebook.com/myliferescue

Instagram: @myliferescue

From Couch to Coach

It seemed so unfair. I had only just got my life back on track after escaping an abusive relationship and starting over again with nothing. I now had a lovely home, a job I loved and a new boyfriend who I adored. Life was good! Until it wasn't…

After months of tests and hospital visits, I'd finally been diagnosed with M.E. (Myalgic Encephalomyelitis) also known as Chronic Fatigue Syndrome. I'd gone from a busy life full of socialising and travelling the country for work, to effectively being house bound. This just felt so unfair.

At the time it was a huge shock, but with hindsight the signs had been there for a while. Knowing what I know now about M.E., I was the perfect candidate. I'd had glandular fever when I was 18 – twice! This led to frequent tonsillitis throughout my adulthood – I thought only kids got that. Each bout needed antibiotics and gradually my immune system started to crack under the pressure.

Another factor that is thought to contribute to M.E. is prolonged periods of stress or unhappiness; I could tick that box too. Years of extreme misery with my verbally abusive (now ex) husband meant I'd lived with that horrible feeling of dread in my gut for far too long. Add to that a job that sent me travelling around the country every week – often with very early starts and late finishes – and unfortunately, I hit the M.E. jackpot. The wonderful life I'd re-built for myself suddenly felt as though it was slipping away.

It could have been worse, of course. I didn't have a terminal illness and my body was pretty much intact (once it had rejected my tonsils and appendix as part of my ongoing decline). One of the most frustrating things about a diagnosis like mine, was the lack of anything anyone could offer to make it go away. There was no magic pill to pop or fixed timescale to work through until I was cured. Nobody could give me any reassurance at all. This was back in 2010. Although M.E. was fairly well known, it was far from well understood and the help and support available was really still very poor.

I was one of the lucky ones. My GP took my condition seriously and referred me to the pain management clinic at my local hospital. I didn't have any pain, but at the time that was the only part of the National Health Service that had any understanding of M.E. Even they couldn't offer me much hope or help. The only thing they offered was group Cognitive Behavioural Therapy (CBT). I grabbed the opportunity and booked in for the next available group session.

I'd read about CBT and understood that it was a talking therapy. The theory being that discussing how I was feeling, along with other M.E. patients, would help me to cope with my symptoms a little better. I was so full of optimism when I arrived at the class. Little did I know that it would indeed be one of the first things that really made a difference, setting me on my path to recovery. But not in the way that they'd intended!

I walked into the session that day, into a dimly lit bare room containing a circle of hard plastic chairs (the kind used in hospital waiting rooms), and the best word I could use to describe the atmosphere was 'bleak'. There were about a dozen people sitting in those chairs and everything about them said 'victim'.

Their body language, their tone of voice, the words they used. Those poor people had been experiencing the hardship of M.E. for years; some of them for more than a decade. Their stories were difficult to hear. None of them were able to work anymore, many of them had to rely on mobility aids to get around and several had broken up with their partners.

I sat there watching and listening, terrified out of my mind that this was the future I had ahead of me. And, right then, I felt this overwhelming surge of determination and positivity settle over me. I thought to myself, "Nope, no way. That is NOT going to be me." I left that session with absolute determination that I was going to beat this.

And I did!

But it wasn't easy, or fast. The first thing I did was talk to my GP again to gain their agreement to sign me off work for a while. There are a number of factors that I credit for my recovery; one of the first was the fact that I was lucky enough to work for a very supportive organisation. They gave me an extended period of sick leave to allow me to focus on my recovery, while not having to worry about money.

That time was so precious to me and I was determined to use it wisely. My energy levels were so low by then that I struggled to leave the house at all. I did, however, have my laptop at home and immediately set about researching things that would help.

At this stage I need to mention my wonderful boyfriend again. Firstly because of his help in supporting me in my continued research for things to try, but mainly just for being him. We'd only been together for a year when I was diagnosed and I was so worried that I was going to lose him. After all, who wants a girlfriend who can't leave the house? And that worry was one of the things that kept me utterly determined to recover as the months and years went on.

With his help – and the love and support of my wonderful family and circle of friends - bit by bit, I started my journey to recovery.

The first stage was learning how to cope. After all, I didn't even know if it was possible to recover at that stage. It was all about how I could learn to cope with the various symptoms and how to use my available energy more wisely. As I started to become more in tune with my body and recognise the signs, I gradually started to be able to do more. I'd still have 'crashes', the periods of days or weeks where your body just 'gives up' and you end up sofa or bed-bound. Over time they became less frequent and less debilitating.

Alongside this focus on pacing my energy, staying positive and never – ever – giving up hope, I started to investigate and try some healing therapies. My hope was that they'd help me move from coping to recovering. I discovered reflexology and found it so helpful that I still go for regular sessions now. I improved my diet, gave up sugar (that was tough!) and took so many supplements that I'm sure I rattled.

This was all about giving my body the help it needed to repair and re-energise itself.

As time went by, I also became more confident in finding creative ways to cope and one example stands out. Even when I was well enough to leave the house, I had to walk everywhere at a snail's pace. Which was fine most of the time - I just shuffled along and let people overtake me. When I needed to use the local zebra crossing, I would worry that the drivers were sitting there getting more and more frustrated as they watched me slowly shuffling along. After all, I didn't look ill; I looked fine! So, I came up with the clever idea of developing a limp when I was crossing the road. It made me feel less concerned, as I knew I'd get sympathy for my non-existent leg injury!

Slowly but surely, this dual approach of carefully pacing myself and nourishing my body started to help my recovery. Don't get me wrong, it was a long and often frustrating journey and I often slipped backwards for a period of time. But focusing on staying positive throughout, coupled with my sense of humour, got me through the tough times. Indeed, my positive attitude was acknowledged as a key factor in my recovery by my hospital consultant in the discharge letter to my GP.

After three years, I felt as though I'd got a decent semblance of a life back. After four I remember thinking, "Well, if this is as good as it gets, I'll take it." After six I was well enough to go on an amazing US/Canadian holiday with my partner, during which he proposed to me in New York's Grand Central Station. The wedding was booked for March 2017 and I achieved my determined ambition to be well enough to enjoy every second of it.

By early 2018 people were asking if I'd completely recovered. I didn't know what to say. I didn't even know if it was possible to completely recover from M.E., but I felt well, energetic and strong. It was this strength that started to push me in a new direction. Now that I was feeling so much better, I looked back at the early stages of my diagnosis and was so grateful for the support of my family, friends and colleagues.

I have no doubt that without that support it would have been so much more of a struggle. I was also very aware that not everyone has such help; many are tackling their recovery alone. As the months passed, my urge to help these people grew and grew. Eventually, I took a six-month sabbatical from my corporate job, while I figured out what the future held. Within a year of my return I'd left my career of 30+ years to follow my heart and support people going through what I had.

That brings me to today. It's been ten years since my diagnosis and it feels wonderful to be following my own passions. I now run my own business helping people achieve their wellbeing goals and ambitions. Although I love helping a variety of people, I'm never more fulfilled than when I'm working with people who want to make a difference for themselves and are tackling recovery from M.E. I've built a coaching framework based on my own recovery success and just knowing that my story is inspiring and helping others is an amazing feeling.

I rescued my wonderful life and I'm going to make the most of every day! If I can, I hope you can too!

SARAH TOMPSETT

Sarah Tompsett is a Kinesiology Practitioner and lives in North Bristol with her husband, two children and her cockapoo, Cooper.

She runs Sarah Tompsett Kinesiology and takes a natural and holistic approach to health. She focuses on the 'whole person' and sees the body and mind as one integrated entity.

Sarah has a particular interest in energy medicine and is also a qualified Reiki Master Practitioner and Munay Ki Graduate.

From Caterpillar to Butterfly is representative of two things. One will become apparent in her journey and the other meaning derives from her practice's logo. Her logo represents the natural shape of the thyroid and the blue wings represent the throat chakra colour.

Facebook: www.facebook.com/sarahtompsettkinesiology

Website: www.sarahtompsettkinesiology.co.uk

Instagram: @sarahtompsettkinesiology

From Caterpillar to Butterfly

In the years before receiving the diagnosis, I was doing what I thought was expected of me. I hadn't given much thought to the way my life was panning out and whether it was in alignment with my authentic self. Just as so many of us do, I was following the crowd and looking to others for validation that I was on the right path.

In reality I'd been on this same bandwagon since school. From senior school to getting my language degree, I'd enjoyed learning and studying. After graduation I worked in London for a recruitment training company, which led to a few years working as a Recruitment Consultant.

It was after moving to Bristol and having met my future husband here, when I began to realise that, what had lit me up when studying and practicing languages, was in fact the ability to connect with many different people. Recruitment as a role lacked that real connection with others and was too sales target focused for me to feel like I was adding any lasting value to anyone.

Cue my move into the wider world of HR. I began to feel connected to a greater purpose and could see the tangible influence this role could have on making life in the workplace better for my colleagues.

Next stop on the bandwagon: marriage, children (I have two, a girl and a boy) and life as a working Mum in the corporate world.

I was DOING ALL THE THINGS! Holding down a Senior HR position, being a Mum, doing school runs, parent's evenings, plays, parties, cooking, cleaning, shopping, going to the gym, dashing around, keeping all the plates spinning.

Sounds great doesn't it? The reality was a never-ending to-do list. Something had to give.

That something was me.

At the start of 2011, I began to feel more tired than I'd ever felt. Not just physically tired but a kind of behind the eyes tired. People would reassure me that this was normal considering the demands on me but somewhere deep down I knew that it was far from normal. This was not the tired I'd been before; this was something else.

On a few separate occasions during the January, I'd fallen asleep whilst playing cars or dinosaurs on the carpet with my little boy. I'd wake up each time having lost 15 or 20 minutes. Thankfully, he hadn't moved but the worry of what could have happened whilst I was asleep pushed me to go to the doctors and find out what was going on. Although part of me didn't want to know.

A few vials of blood were taken to rule out various conditions such as anaemia, celiac disease and underactive thyroid. The wait for the results seemed endless. I was worried there was something seriously wrong with me.

The answer came while I was sitting at the side of the swimming pool, watching one of my children in their swimming lesson. The doctor called with the diagnosis: Hashimoto's.

I had never heard of it! To explain, Hashimoto's is an autoimmune disorder that can cause an underactive thyroid or hypothyroidism; in fact it is the most common cause of hypothyroidism and primarily affects women. The doctor confirmed that the condition was at Stage 3, the subclinical stage, which means that the disease was not severe enough to show obvious symptoms. Two of the thyroid hormones (T4 and T3) were in the 'normal' range and a third hormone, Thyroid Stimulating Hormone (TSH), was slightly elevated. Autoimmunity was confirmed with a fourth hormone, Thyroid Peroxidase (TPO) Antibodies. The antibodies attack the thyroid gland and cause inflammation and impaired function of the thyroid.

It was the autoimmune element of the diagnosis that hit me the hardest.

I'd always looked after myself in terms of nutrition and exercise. I didn't drink a lot of alcohol (post babies) and I'd never smoked. Despite my relatively healthy lifestyle, I felt like my body had let me down. In my naivety at the time, I thought that autoimmunity meant the body was attacking itself.

Having spent years since researching and learning about autoimmunity, I now know that the body is only ever trying to protect us. Autoimmunity is not the body attacking itself; rather a sign that the body is trying to keep safe by switching things around a little. I believe (and there is research to back this up) that the body is caught in a loop of stress. Unless we listen to what it is telling us, it won't be able to do its best work: to self-heal.

Looking back, I can see that the way I rushed around unable to switch off, coupled with my perfectionist tendencies, had put my nervous system into a constant state of fight or flight. My sympathetic nervous system was always in 'go' mode. I'm not sure I ever got much time in the rest and restoration state. It is during the rest and restoration state that the body is able to begin the healing process by engaging its parasympathetic nervous system.

The doctor suggested I start medication, but I was hesitant given what I had read. Bear in mind that I still had options because the condition was in the 'subclinical' stage, so I am not saying my approach and decision to not medicate is right for everyone. It just didn't make sense to me. The medication offered was a synthetic replacement hormone (T4); the standard 'treatment' for underactive thyroid. I had normal levels of T4 in my body, so logically I couldn't see how it was going to help me get well.

I wanted to know how to lower the Thyroid Stimulating Hormone levels and the thyroid antibodies that were up in the 900s at the time. After some time spent researching this myself, it seemed there wasn't a simple solution. Rather it would take a combination of several things together to help reverse the antibody count and put the condition into remission.

I discovered that autoimmunity is not something that will ever go away. It is created by a 'perfect storm' of contributing factors coming together. Three of the key factors are; genetics (some people are predisposed to autoimmunity), the environment (think stress and how you react emotionally to that stress) and gut health; namely leaky gut, also known as intestinal permeability.

The diagnosis felt like a warning; an opportunity to start a journey of self-discovery. Something inside me, call it intuition or a gut feeling, told me that this would be the path to helping me understand the connection between my body and mind. More importantly, this would be the path to healing and finding who out who I was.

From a young age, I have been interested in and drawn to spirituality and energy work. I received Reiki 1 and 2 attunements some years before the diagnosis and was attuned to Reiki Master level a few years after. What I'd learned on my Reiki journey allowed me to address my health from an energetic perspective as well as delving deep into my emotions using self-enquiry techniques. I started regularly practicing Reiki on myself, holding my hands over my thyroid. I visualised it healed and my body healthy.

To get well on all levels, I knew I had to take a completely holistic approach. One of the biggest breakthroughs for me was being introduced to Kinesiology through a good friend. I hadn't heard of it before, but I was interested to see how it may help my body to reverse the condition. Kinesiology uses muscle response testing to get biochemical feedback from the body and finds the imbalances that are at the root of your health issues. The body is brought back into balance using a series of techniques so that it can begin the process of self-healing.

As expected, kinesiology showed that my adrenals were exhausted. No surprise there given how I had rushed around for years! Absolute priority for me was managing and lowering my stress levels. I needed to give my body a chance to get into the rest and restoration state as often as possible.

I also had leaky gut; another common symptom found in people with autoimmune conditions. There were some foods that I was intolerant to that needed to come out of my diet. Gluten was one of those foods; an irritant for anyone with a thyroid condition (and many other conditions besides). Muscle testing highlighted relevant nutritional supplements that would give me a boost of the vitamins and minerals my body was low in as well as healing the leaky gut.

Each time I had kinesiology I would leave my session knowing my body was back in balance and able to start healing itself. I was amazed at how my body responded once I listened to it and committed to using the tools it needed. The continued lowering of the antibody count was a great tangible marker of things moving in the right direction.

It must be said that working with my body naturally was not a quick or easy fix but I have always been in it for the long haul and committed to getting well.

Below is a list of the tools I still continue to use for my wellbeing. These have become routine for me and I will engage in at least one or two on the list whenever I feel overwhelm starting to creep in:

Listen to your body: Being in constant fight or flight mode will catch up with you at some point so listen to the whispers before they become screams!

Get to know your stress triggers.

All disease starts in the gut (Hippocrates) so look after your gut by nourishing it.

Feel your emotions. Don't push them down or bottle them up.

Leave toxic work environments.

Set your boundaries. Don't say yes when you mean no (note: this one gets easier the more you do it!)

Never compare yourself to others. We are all on our own journey.

Use affirmations. My favourite is 'All is well' by Louise Hay, the queen of affirmations

Meditate, even if just for 2 minutes at a time.

Practice journaling.

Sleep: Get at least 7-8 hours a night and be asleep before 11pm.

Realise that you are not alone! There are a number of amazing therapies and therapists out there to get your body back into balance.

Get regular balancing through kinesiology to give your body the best chance to self-heal.

Do what lights you up!

At the end of the day, the diagnosis of Hashimoto's led me to Kinesiology and for that I will be forever grateful. In fact, who knew I'd be so in awe of Kinesiology and natural healthcare that I would start my own Kinesiology and wellbeing practice? I am sure that doing what I am passionate about helps to keep me well.

I am humbled to have the privilege of supporting people on their journeys to wellness as I continue on mine. Nothing is more rewarding than seeing their positive outcomes.

My intent in writing this chapter is that it gives hope to someone else with an autoimmune condition. Know that your body is ALWAYS working FOR you and its ability to heal is greater than you have ever imagined.

Warm wishes,

Sarah

STACEY MARTIN

Stacey Martin is a fun-loving, very sociable, bubbly, ambitious independent woman who became a bank manager by the age of 21

Stacey is now a mortgage adviser by day and DJ by night. Stacey lives her life at 100mph with a "strike while the iron is hot" attitude. Stacey is a go getter, her glass is always a half full, she takes everything in her stride with a smile on her face.

Stacey is very family orientated with a big heart and despite her hectic lifestyle always finds time for anyone and everyone.

Two More Pushes

As it got to the 19th hour my midwife looked at me and smiled, "Two more pushes and your baby will be here, you're about to become a Mum"

I'll never be able to describe the relief I felt at that moment. Until two more pushes turned to three, then four, then five.

As more time passed, the less I knew what was going on.

"Push!" She said again.

Then she shouted to my husband to hit the emergency button.

From that moment on the danger increased. Both me and my daughter were at serious risk of not surviving this.

Doctors were rushing in, all in a complete frenzy trying to decide what to do in order to keep both of us alive.

My daughter was too low down for a Caesarean and the forceps couldn't bring her out either. In my fragile state my body was unable to respond with any one emotion. I wasn't crying, screaming, or shaking. I was just still, cold and emotionless; watching a nightmare unfold thinking, "I'll wake up soon. This isn't really happening to me it's must be a bad dream."

"There's no longer a heartbeat." I hear the doctors say.

More panic, more doctors using all their power and knowledge to save my baby's life.

56 minutes later, the rotational forceps successfully pulled my baby out, but the danger wasn't over. I see the back of a blue baby pulled from me. A cord wrapped around her neck; limp, floppy, silent and completely lifeless.

The doctors and nurses used all at their disposal to bring her back to life. The worst 42 minutes of my life yet, until finally I feel my midwifes hand on mine and hear her say "We have a heartbeat."

This wasn't a Hollywood movie; this wasn't the end and my nightmare wasn't over yet. In reality my baby still wasn't in my arms, her life was still in danger. She had to be put on life support and taken to the intensive care unit.

At this point I too was still in danger. I was losing a lot of blood and the last thing I remember was telling my husband to go with our daughter before falling unconscious.

As I woke, I was safe again, but my baby was on life support. She had two collapsed lungs torn away from the walls, suspected meningitis B and a weak heart.

While she was in intensive care, I couldn't experience any of the early magic; holding your baby for the first time, looking her in the eye and naming her. I had names in mind but needed to see her before I knew it felt right. Without a name she sat in intensive care, with a hospital number as an identity.

I missed out on all the firsts. The first nappy, the first feed or the first outfit. Instead, there were doctors and consultants everywhere, all telling us different things, all talking in medical jargon; most of which I didn't understand. I just had to sit and watch. I placed my hands on the edge of the incubator to get as close to her as I possibly could.

To my relief, after 4 days in intensive care I got to hold her for the first time. This amazing feeling was short-lived as she suddenly stopped breathing again. I was dragged out of intensive care by a nurse and left watching as a team of doctors tried to resuscitate her.

Eventually, as the days went on, my nightmare finally ended. Maisie started to improve each day until we were told we could finally go home. As we were leaving, the doctor told us something which still to this day leaves me with goosebumps, "It's a miracle you both survived and are walking out of here in one piece."

My baby may be safe, but my body was not in one piece

6 months later – I was back in the hospital told by the gynaecologist, "You have severe nerve damage". This explained why I was in constant pain. Even sitting down hurt. The pain was so bad that something as simple as getting in and out of a car would make my eyes water. I couldn't endure this

any longer and needed surgery. I was confidently told there was a 95% success rate and a less than 1% risk of causing any further damage or pain. The odds were in my favour, so I took my chances and agreed. I was cut, re-stitched and had all the nerve damage removed.

Unfortunately, the operation wasn't a success; in fact it couldn't have gone any worse and I was left in the 1% of people who then experienced more pain. In addition, I was also suffering from lots of internal damage caused by the rotational forceps.

Whilst I was recovering from the failed operation, I had to brace myself for all the procedures lined up to fix my internals. I had 17 trips to the hospital in under 11 weeks. Each trip involved being put through an hour of excruciating pain whilst physios tried to realign my insides. I would dread each appointment; I knew the pain that was coming.

It was during those session I would channel my thoughts into thinking how lucky I was to have a daughter who survived. I would tell myself I can take whatever pain or procedure I have to, because nothing in my whole life will ever be as painful, as the first time I saw my daughter in intensive care. I will forever be haunted by the fact I had to ask which baby was mine. I had never had the chance to see her face before this, so I was unable to recognise her.

At this point my life was lived in and out of the hospital. I approached my employers and asked if I could reduce my hours on medical grounds but was told by my male boss that it was not possible. I asked to speak with a female manager. There weren't any female managers in my department available to me, so the answer was no.

I was devastated. I worked for the same bank since I was 17 years old. It was the only company I had ever worked for. In my hour of need at 28 years of age, after more than 11 years of service with them they were not interested in helping me. I was made to feel like I had no option other than to quit, so I did. I didn't have the fight in me at the time to take them on or challenge anything as all my energy was being taken up with my medical issues.

Next up was steroid injections straight into my never damage. I ended up having 12 of them over a period of about 12 months. Not one made a single difference and they were excruciatingly painful. To get me through, again I would think of my daughter.

My consultant finally said she was unable to give me anymore. I'd already had more than I should have done.

I wasn't ready to give up yet.

Medication was next, they tried to alter my nervous system to block the pain that way. This didn't work either; I had the two bad side effects. The first side effect was uncontrollable shaking. I lost the ability to control my hands, they would constantly shake and I had no way of stopping it. These episodes were sudden and I had no idea how long they would last. This terrified me. It was at least 8 – 10 times a day lasting from 10 minutes to an hour.

The second side effect was hair loss. My hair started to fall out in clumps. I have long, thick brown hair and often receive compliments; it's probably my best feature. Every time I brushed it or washed it in the shower, I would see it disappear down the plughole. I felt like a broken woman, unable to control what was happening to my body.

As the medication didn't help with the pain, I was taken off of it. Luckily for me the shaking stopped and my hair grew back over time.

The consultants were running out of options. "You need to come to terms with the fact you are likely to spend the rest of your life in constant pain. You need to talk to someone about the fact you and your husband are not likely to ever be intimate again."

We were sent for psychosexual counselling. The counsellor was amazing, a really lovely lady. I'll never forget how kind and caring she was, it really helped.

I also got a second and third opinion from private health case consultants. They had no other suggestions and the only option left was to operate again.

"What are the odds of it working?" I asked.

Not that It really mattered. Every single odd had gone against me.

"I don't know. I will either make you pain free or put you in more pain."

I thought about it for a minute. "Go for it." I said. "I'm in constant pain now, I'll take the risk of being in more pain for the chance of being pain free."

She looked nervous. Two weeks later I had the operation done again.

Within 3 weeks it was obvious it hadn't worked. The pain was worse than ever before.

"I'm so sorry" said my consultant "I have to discharge you, there's nothing else I can do," she said with tears rolling from her eyes.

We had gotten to know each other really well. She had been looking after me for over 3 years. She gave me her personal phone number and said If I ever needed anything, to give her a call. I left her room and walked down the hospital corridor for the final time. It had been over 3 years since the first time I walked in and I was leaving in more pain than ever.

When I met people for coffee or saw them in passing, they wouldn't say, "Hiya, how are you?" They would ask, "Hey, how's your fanny?" Talking about it helped to get it off my chest!

One day someone suggested trying Reiki. I had nothing to lose and on a plus side, Reiki wasn't going to be painful like all the other procedures I had gone through. I had one session every three weeks.

Within 6 sessions I started to notice a difference. I sat down one evening and didn't wince in pain. Gradually over time the pain diminished and I was able to start getting back to normal. After 10 months of regular Reiki I was able to have sex again.

One year later I spoke to my doctor.

"How can I help you today?" She asked.

"I've got honeymoon cystitis. I've had too much sex!"

"Say that again?" She said; there was excitement in her voice.

I told her again, I was so proud. "I'm no longer in pain. I can have sex!! I've had loads of it, every day!!! And now I've got cystitis!!"

"I'm so pleased for you!" she said "What lovely news! I'll send an antibiotic prescription to the chemist for you. What a turnaround! How has this happened?" She asked.

"Reiki" I told her. "Reiki healed me! I had it for a year and the pain has gone. I've stopped taking all the medication. I am pain free, I'm as good as new. I literally can't believe it."

I also sent a text to my lovely consultant, *"I'm no longer in any pain. I also have honeymoon cystitis from too much shagging, making up for lost time. Thanks for everything you did over the past few years."*

Her reply was, *"Proud of you, no one else deserves the cystitis as much as you! Thanks for the lovely message, it's made my day x"*

Over the last few years I've learnt all that matters in life is your health and happiness. I nearly died 2 weeks after my 28th birthday on an operating table whilst giving birth to my daughter. I was told statistically there was more chance of my daughter dying that surviving. I didn't realise until 2 years later that my odds weren't much higher.

I will always feel robbed of that special magical moment and I will never get over the fact I had to ask which baby was mine when I first got to see my daughter in intensive care. However I do believe everything happens for a reason. I now know if you put your mind to something and you are determined enough, you can make it happen. I have proved this to myself.

I could have sat on my sofa, in pain, feeling sorry for myself. I didn't. I was adamant I was going to recover, so I refused to give up. When I did recover, I bounced back stronger, tougher, happier and more confident than I ever could have imagined.

VALERIE CRITCHLOW

Val is a go-getting mother of two and a grandmother. Raised in the West Country she started life at an outdoor school because of her breathing issues.

Despite her start in life she became a business woman and rallied 90 local businesses to reignite a trading association which she chaired for many years. When the economic downturn took its toll on her business she followed her first love of caring and embarked on a new career.

Now retired, Val is a Director of the housing development where she lives and still lives by the principal that "If you want a job doing well, do it yourself."

If You Want A Job Done Properly, Do It Yourself!

When asked to write a small piece on overcoming life's challenges I was happy to do it, but wondered what I had done to warrant inclusion. I mentally went through some of the jobs that I had done in my life and realised I had a story to tell. By the time I was in my late forties I'd had my two wonderful children, I had worked as a waitress in a hotel, ran a small restaurant and then worked in a shop selling corsetry. I liked this so much that I asked the owner if I could train with her to make the corsets. I enjoyed it at first, but found that it wasn't challenging enough, so I took the plunge; I leased a shop and sold fashion.

I had fun organising fashion shows to raise money for local charities and getting my friends to join in as models. I also fitted bras for unfortunate ladies who had had lumpectomies and mastectomies. I even went to the local hospital to reassure ladies that life can go on after breast cancer. Trading was getting harder and so, alongside another small business, we built up a local trading association to attract people to our area of town. In total we engaged with over 90 local businesses. I chaired Torre Traders for several years, but by now it was the late 1980's and the recession hit my business. I tried to keep the business going but could not go on and so I declared myself bankrupt.

I lived in a seaside town where tourism, the main industry, had already suffered with the advent of cheap foreign holidays. Plus with the current economic climate taking effect, hotel and restaurant jobs, the main standby for working people in such towns, were in short supply. Before I had my first child I had wanted to be a nurse, but in the 1960's it wasn't usual to go in to that type of role when you were married with a child. When I put on my thinking cap, I realised that there were many Residential Care Homes in the area. Being a popular place for older retirees, these were unlikely to be so badly hit by recession. So I could finally get the opportunity to try the caring role I had once wanted.

I had no experience of caring for the elderly in a professional capacity, but I had looked after older family members in the past, so I was confident that I could handle the less agreeable aspects of the job. I applied for and landed a job as an assistant in a home for residents with Alzheimer's and Dementia.

I took to the job immediately but soon realised that the standard of care and respect for the residents fell far short of what I was expecting. Not being one to hold my opinions to myself, I voiced my concerns to the management. Not surprisingly, they took exception and I left by mutual consent. I took jobs in a couple of other homes where standards were better, but still not where I would be happy to leave a close relative of mine. In one Home the owner had left a pane of glass in the office. I fell against it and received a serious injury to my hand. My local hospital was unable to treat it and I was shipped off 35 miles to Plymouth to be repaired. I had no wish to go back to that Home - in retrospect I could probably have successfully sued them. After 15 weeks off I was able to start looking again and things began to look up.

The new Home I went to was good. The staff and food were of a much better standard and I really took to it. The residents suffered from strokes, Alzheimer's and Dementia. I worked for 6 months and was then made a senior, having taken the N.V.Q exams. I was so proud but by now I was heading towards 50. I had my mother living with me and I gradually noticed that she was developing Dementia. I sorted her out with day care and respite and I took care of her in the evenings and overnight. I carried on working in the Home I had grown to love and 6 months down the road the manager left and I was asked if I would like to become the manager. Needless to say I accepted! The staff were happy and we created such a great atmosphere that soon staff from other Homes were applying for jobs. Having worked with them in the past, I knew their qualities - one I made my deputy and two more I made seniors. I was finally at the top of my career and loving it. I worked in that job for 11years before retiring.

If I could change career at a later stage in life, so can you.

In retirement my life took a further turn. Understanding the needs of the vulnerable and the infirm has been my life's work and with great surprise I was invited to join the Board of the flats where I now live. Matching what the residents need to the cash available and giving attention to those who do not have a voice has become my new career. Maybe I won't retire at all!

AFTERWORD

by Sharon Critchlow

Thank you for reading this book. The chapters were all written by people like you and me and it takes courage to show your scars to the world. We thank all of our authors for sharing their stories and hope that as the Reader you are left with feelings of hope and inspiration.

Story telling has its foundation in ancient times when we lived a more communal life. Stories were shared around the campfire to serve as warnings, inspirations and to remember our history. To reflect on good outcomes, to mould our thoughts and to highlight our similarities with those who have walked this path before - and survived.

In this book we have embraced our body image, moved on from bankruptcy and struggled with our health. We have travelled to foreign lands and learned to thrive, survived strokes, and experienced physical attacks. We have loved, lost, overcome depression and learned to love ourselves.

We have experienced IVF, nearly died giving life to our children and adopted the children of others. We have both valued our experience within motherhood and discovered joy in a childless life.

All of life has been here.

Some of these chapters may resonate more with you today than others. If you open this book next year, stories may emerge as relevant for you at that time. The human journey is a reflective one. Each of us seeing our experiences replayed and our fears faced in the lives of those around us.

If you have been affected by a particular chapter in this book, we ask that you talk to someone: a friend, your GP or a specialist. A trouble shared is a trouble halved as they say and you will hear that in our author's stories they were able to overcome their challenges, however great.

In this book we see that whatever our trauma in life, our feelings and our emotions are the same as everyone who has been here before us. To be human is reflect those feelings as that is our collective history because to be human is to love and through love we can all thrive. Thank you.

ABOUT DISCOVER YOUR BOUNCE!

Discover Your Bounce has emerged as a group of companies to provide a platform for wellbeing, to support each other and to learn from our collective experience.

Discover Your Bounce Publishing specialises in inspirational stories and business books. We provide mentoring for authors and support from inception of your idea to cheerleading your book launch. If you have an idea for a book or a part written manuscript that you want to get over the line contact Nicky or Sharon on the links below.

Discover Your Bounce For Business provides support for employers who want to improve the staff wellbeing, engagement, culture and performance of their business. We work with CEOs, HR Managers or department heads to create practical, easy to implement techniques that create instant change. As we go to print we have worked with over 2000 employees across the country from a variety of industries and have delivered keynotes at some fantastic international conferences and events.

Discover Your Bounce Lifestyle has for the past 7 years worked with individuals through mentoring and our online courses to improve their energy and vision. If your get up and go has got up and gone get in touch and get bouncing!

Sharon and Nicky are available to discuss speaking opportunities, wellbeing workshops or private mentoring:

Nicky@discoveryourbounce.com or Sharon@discoveryourbounce.com

You can also find out more on our website: www.discoveryourbounce.com

JOIN US!

You are now part of our community and we would love you to join our Facebook group – The Discover Your Bounce Community.

Printed in Great Britain
by Amazon